"It is so easy to settle into our personalities and preferences and surrender to 'that's-just-the-way-I-am-and-I-can't-change.' But when we do, we find that the Spirit is constantly at work pointing out the gaps between this approach and all that the gospel calls us to be. *Both/And Ministry* not only points out the gaps we may have become blind to; it also energizes us for ongoing repentance and faith until the day when all of the gaps are gone for good."

Nancy Guthrie, Bible teacher;
Author, *Blessed* and *Even Better Than Eden*

"With a heart for those who exercise any kind of Christian ministry or leadership, Millar writes with compassion, encouragement and insight to guide his readers into the joy of both Jesus' completed work for us and his continual work in us. *Both/And Ministry* does more than call out the error of the Christian 'pendulum swing' that constantly oscillates between two half-truths—it directs us into fullness of life in Christ."

Kanishka Raffel, Archbishop of Sydney

"In a day of soundbites and hype, this book comes as a refreshing word of sanity. Gary Millar shows the multicoloured nature of Christian life and ministry, and refuses to allow it to become monochrome. He helps us grasp the different angles of Jesus' teaching and resist the temptation to boil them down to just one thing. We all need 'both/and' ministry."

Graham Beynon, Head of Local Ministries, FIEC UK

T0284202

"It takes a particular talent to accomplish what Gary Millar has done in this characteristically clear and profoundly helpful book. With a lightness of touch he helps us understand the keys to living a life truly grounded in the gospel and pursuing a ministry genuinely shaped by that gospel."

Alistair Begg, Bible Teacher at Truth For Life; Senior Pastor, Parkside Church, Cleveland, OH, Author, *Pray Big* and *Brave by Faith*

"Distinctly Christian integrity insists that we hold the 'both/and' concepts of our faith in a perpetual bear hug. With gracious wisdom and candid explanations, our friend Gary teaches us how to do just that. You'll be both encouraged and challenged by this book."

Gloria Furman, Author, *Treasuring Christ When Your Hands Are Full* and *The Pastor's Wife*

"I absolutely love how gospel-centred this book is! As a result, it is both deeply humbling and wonderfully liberating at the same time. Read it to be refreshed and rejuvenated to serve Christ fervently again."

Denesh Divyanathan, Senior Pastor, The Crossing Church, Singapore; Chairman, Evangelical College of Asia (Singapore)

"Christ is only our representative Savior. Or Christ is our example to follow. Why do these two have to be divided? My good friend Gary Millar challenges stalemates such as this with his usual pastoral and theological wisdom. This book should be read as widely as possible!"

Michael Horton, J. Gresham Machen Professor of Systematic Theology and Apologetics, Westminster Seminary, CA

"A realistic and gracious book that helps you better understand God's character, his work, and who you are— and that helps you better reconcile the paradox that although living as a Christian is difficult at times, it is a life full of joy. Gary Millar has written an immensely practical book that will bless many as they are convicted and comforted by our Lord Jesus Christ."

Jane Tooher, Director of the Priscilla & Aquila Centre, Moore Theological College, Sydney

"In this warm and wise book, Gary Millar makes sense of the many apparent tensions of ministry and leadership, reminding us that as disciples of Christ, we are called to 'a life that is marked by contrasts and paradoxes that reflect the glorious richness of our God and Saviour'. Gary helps us to recognise, navigate and value the many 'both/and' realities we encounter when we seek to live and lead like Jesus. A great personal or team read for facilitating reflection on ministry and growth in ministry."

Jen Charteris, Executive Director, Crosslands Training

Both / And

LIVING AND LEADING
LIKE JESUS

Ministry

GARY MILLAR

thegoodbook
COMPANY

Both/And Ministry: Living and Leading Like Jesus

© Gary Millar, 2025

Published by:
The Good Book Company

thegoodbook.com | thegoodbook.co.uk
thegoodbook.com.au | thegoodbook.co.nz | thegoodbook.co.in

Unless otherwise noted, all Scripture quotations are taken from the
Christian Standard Bible, Anglicised Edition, Copyright © 2024 by Holman
Bible Publishers. Used by permission. Christian Standard Bible and CSB are
federally registered trademarks of Holman Bible Publishers.

All emphases in Scripture quotations have been added by the author.

All rights reserved. Except as may be permitted by the Copyright Act, no
part of this publication may be reproduced in any form or by any means
without prior permission from the publisher.

Gary Millar has asserted his right under the Copyright, Designs and Patents
Act 1988 to be identified as author of this work.

Design by Drew McCall

ISBN: 9781802541267 | JOB-007938 | Printed in India

Contents

On Playing the Didgeridoo (and Living a Genuinely Gospel-Shaped Life)

The secret to playing the didgeridoo—one of the classic instruments of the indigenous peoples of Australia—is, apparently, learning to breathe in and breathe out *at the same time*. Both of those actions are actually pretty simple. In fact, you could say that they come naturally! For our whole lives, we manage to breathe in and then breathe out and breathe in again with a reassuring regularity. But try to do them at the same time (I dare you!) and it's a very different matter.

I have now been a Christian for over 40 years, and I've come to the conclusion that living for the Lord Jesus is a bit like playing the didgeridoo. It's basically a matter of doing some pretty simple things *at the same time*. Things like learning to live confidently in Christ *and* mistrust our own sinfulness; or being urgent about gospel work *and* patient with people; or taking up our cross and denying ourselves daily *and* running to Jesus to find rest for our souls. If we could separate these things out, focusing on one of them at a time, they would be relatively straightforward. The challenge is that we have to do these basic things all at the same time. Living the Christian life—this "both/and" kind of life—isn't really all that complicated; it's just hard!

That's just as true when it comes to the particular focus of this book: doing gospel ministry. If you are part of the body of Christ, you are (or should be) involved in ministry at some level—by which I basically mean doing stuff at church. Whether it's cleaning the toilets or writing Bible-study material, making Play-Doh models with the pre-schoolers or preaching on Habakkuk to the adults—it's all ministry. But I suspect that the more responsibility in church life you have, the more important this book will feel—because the damage done by getting it wrong increases.

You see, when it comes to living and leading like Jesus, we don't get to pick and choose which of his commands to follow. Being gifted in one area (say, preaching) doesn't make up for being harsh or selfish towards your team. Gentleness is a beautiful trait, but it doesn't get us off the hook when it comes to having difficult but necessary conversations with those we love for their good. Christian ministry is an all-embracing, both/and kind of thing. If we don't take that seriously, sooner or later, it will lead to disaster.

Perhaps you've witnessed that type of disaster first-hand in the failure of a Christian leader. You might be aware of global figures. Or you may well know of other, less famous individuals whose downfall nonetheless created havoc and disappointment in the local churches and ministries of which they were a part. The individual circumstances were different, but they all had this in common: the individual overlooked or ignored or excused themselves from living for Jesus in one or more key areas of the Christian life as described plainly in the Bible.

Of course, it shouldn't come as a shock to any of us that such "great ones" could sin. The repeated and dramatic failures of virtually every key figure in the Old Testament make it very clear that even the best of us are only a couple of steps away from sinning spectacularly. The whole Bible is full of blunt statements about our deep-rooted corruption (like Jeremiah 17:9 and Romans 3:23).

But what is surprising is that in almost every case of leadership failure, both the person themselves and many of those closest to them had somehow managed to excuse clearly sinful behaviour for a long time. Great giftedness—or great effectiveness—was valued over basic godliness. These leaders stopped doing some of the essentials—and the result was disaster.

And that's how it works for all of us; we're all called to live godly lives. Not many reading this book will have to demonstrate on the world stage that our words and lives match. Instead, we'll have to do it in the context of our families and our local church family—doing a range of simple things at the same time as we seek to serve Jesus together. This book is about doing just that. It's a book about living a genuinely gospel-shaped, Christ-like life for the rest of our lives.

A Gospel-Shaped Life Is a Christ-Like Life

The most vivid picture we have of the both/and life is the life of the Lord Jesus.

God has given us four rich and nuanced accounts of the life of Jesus. Jesus lived with a poise and vibrancy that is unmatched in human history for he alone is God in the flesh. He was the one who always managed to speak the truth and to love those to whom he spoke; to be gentle and courageous; to be focused on the big picture and compassionate to the person in front of him. Jesus did the basics beautifully, all the time. He is the one who has done what we're talking about in this book perfectly.

But the marvellous thing is that he came both to model the gospel-shaped life and to put it within our reach.

In John's Gospel, Jesus makes the remarkable statement that he came so that we might have "life … in abundance" (John 10:10). The full effect of his incarnation, flawless life, substitutionary death, stunning resurrection and ongoing rule and intercession is to make it possible for us to live *like him*. We need both the picture of this life and the ability to live it— and Jesus provides us with both.

It isn't simply the Gospels which focus on the life which we are enabled to live in Christ. The greater part of the rest of the New Testament was devoted to helping emerging Christian communities across the Mediterranean to live out God's calling. All of Paul's letters, for example, follow essentially the same pattern: the apostle lays out the basic contours of what God has done for us in Christ (for example, Romans 1 – 8; Ephesians 1 – 3) and then moves on to describe a local expression of the gospel-shaped life (Romans 12 – 15; Ephesians 4 – 6). This gospel-shaped life is what this book is all about.

It is written for people, like me, who feel the weight of having to live a joined-up life—of living in a way in which our words and actions match. It's written for people like me who find it hard to do the simple things well, day after day. It's written for people, like me,, who would much prefer to focus on what comes easily to us and forget about the things we find challenging. It's written for people, like me, who want to live like Jesus and know that we need all the help we can get.

As I started to write, I was thinking about those who, like me, have the privilege of being paid to serve the church of the Lord Jesus. But as I got started, I realised that we all face the same basic challenges. So this book is written both for those who usually stand at the front and those who prefer to serve in the background.

If you've ever felt frustrated by your apparent inability to do the simple things that you encourage other people to do, this book is for you. If you've ever stood in front of a group of Christians feeling that you're about to be crushed by the weight of your own hypocrisy, welcome. If you ever feel tempted to justify your weakness (or sin!) in one area by saying, "But at least I do so much better over here", read on. If you find yourself with a great capacity to forget even the most obvious things, then I've written this book to point you once again to the help that God himself has already provided.

This book aims to help you avoid the danger of settling for less than what God offers. It's written to help you spot where you have made bad choices, excused yourself and opted out of an authentically gospel-shaped life. It's an encouragement to pursue the beautiful, Christ-like, Spirit-empowered life of repentance and faith that God has called you to—a life that isn't complicated but is hard. A life that is marked by contrasts and paradoxes that reflect the glorious richness of our God and Saviour.

Most mornings, I read a Puritan-inspired prayer from a collection entitled *The Valley of Vision*. As I was thinking about this whole idea of the often paradoxical both/and life, I reached the end of the book and started again as usual. As I read the very first prayer in the book, this is what I found: I'd invite you to pray this with me as we start our journey together.

Lord, high and holy, meek and lowly,
Thou has brought me to the valley of vision,
where I live in the depths but see Thee in the heights;
hemmed in by mountains of sin I behold Thy glory.

Let me learn by paradox
that the way down is the way up,
that to be low is to be high,
that the broken heart is the healed heart,
that the contrite spirit is the rejoicing spirit,
that the repenting soul is the victorious soul,
that to have nothing is to possess all,
that to bear the cross is to wear the crown,
that to give is to receive, that the valley is the place of
vision.

Lord, in the daytime stars can be seen from deepest wells,
and the deeper the wells the brighter Thy stars shine;
Let me find Thy light in my darkness,
Thy life in my death,
Thy joy in my sorrow,
Thy grace in my sin,
Thy riches in my poverty
Thy glory in my valley.[1]

---

1 Ed. Arthur Bennett, *The Valley of Vision: A Collection of Puritan Prayers &*
   Devotions (Banner of Truth, 1988)

CHAPTER 1

Both/And Theology

When 50% Isn't a Pass

I work in a theological college, and in most of the assessments or exams, the pass mark is 50%. If you get 50%, it isn't great, but it's enough—and you can move on without resitting. But real life isn't quite like that. More often, only doing 50% of what we're supposed to do can lead to all kinds of problems.

There are many times in my life when I've tried to protest that I should get credit for doing half of a job rather than being criticised for not doing it all. Perhaps I did leave the front door open... but I did lock the back door! I may have forgotten to buy milk... but I did pick up the breakfast cereal! I may have forgotten to look left as I drove out the gate... but I did look right! Unfortunately, my defences don't hold up because these situations are all both/and things, where only doing 50% of the job isn't a pass; it's a recipe for disaster. And nowhere is this more obvious than in theology. Biblical theology is a both/and thing. The gospel is a both/and thing. That's why the Christian life is a both/and thing too.

This both/and principle isn't just a catchy slogan or even a handy way to organise how we think about discipleship; it has deep theological roots. It shows us the power and beauty of the message of the gospel, and of God himself.

Capturing the Power and Beauty of the Gospel

We'll need that power and beauty if we're going to avoid feeling crushed. After all, any time we press into just how all-encompassing and demanding life as a Christian really is, we face a problem: we start to feel *bad*. Most of us, most of the time, are *already* quite clear on the fact that we aren't living quite as we should. So the idea of having to come to terms with *extra* ways in which we mess up—perhaps without even realising it—can feel a bit overwhelming. And of course, hearing that Christian ministry is a both/and thing inevitably suggests that we might have to *do* more as a result of reading this book— and few of us are looking for anything more to work on as we follow Jesus!

But don't panic. This book isn't just a glorified to-do list for Christians. To start to think about the both/and life which the gospel calls us to is ultimately to be thrown back on our both/and God. It's to be pressed deeper into the both/and nature of our salvation. And this turns out to be a moving, exciting, humbling, comforting and empowering thing! Behind every encouragement to live differently stands the double conviction that our God is both gloriously different himself *and empowers us to be different*. This theology is the engine that drives everything which follows.

So before we go any further (and start to wrestle with the details of living a both/and life), in the rest of this chapter, we're going to think a little more about our both/and God and our both/and salvation.

The Both/And God

From the beginning of the Bible, God reveals himself to us as a God who specializes in glorious contrasts. He's a both/and God, in all three Persons of the Trinity.

1. THE BOTH/AND FATHER

God is both *transcendent* and *immanent*—in other words, he both sits *above all things* on his heavenly throne and gets *involved in things* in this world, and specifically with people like us. So, no sooner has God created everything in Genesis 1 than he is speaking to Adam in the garden (Genesis 2:16-17). The pattern continues all through the Old Testament: God speaks from heaven but allows his people to hear his voice and taste his presence on earth (Deuteronomy 4:32-40).

Once the Israelites have left Egypt, God instructs them to set up the tabernacle as an earthly replica of his heavenly dwelling and put the Ark of the Covenant, representing his throne, in the middle. He does this so that people will know that he is with Israel—they even see the glory of God descending on the tent in Exodus 40. But they are repeatedly reminded that the ultimate throne of God is in heaven. In Isaiah 6, for example, the prophet gets a glimpse of that throne. As he cranes his neck and looks upward, even the very edge of the robe of the one sitting on that throne fills and overwhelms the temple!

God is both immanent and transcendent: both "in it" with us and "above it all". If he were just one or the other—50%—he wouldn't be much help to us. But as it is, he is the Father who both understands us and is able to come to our aid because he is the all-powerful ruler of the universe.

This then spills over into the fact that God is a God of *glory* and of *grace*.

It's hard to miss the fact that God is blisteringly, superlatively different. He is regularly described with words like "glorious" (which carries the nuance of royal majesty) and "holy" (implying purity and radical differentness). Isaiah 6 again provides the most famous example, as God's heavenly attendants are overheard crying, "Holy, holy, holy is the LORD of Armies; his glory fills the whole earth" (Isaiah 6:3).[2] When characters in the Bible disregard this reality, the results are disastrous—see, for example, the events of Exodus 32, when Israel tried to make God more "manageable" by representing him as a golden calf.

And yet, for every narrative in which people encounter God in consuming purity, there is one in which God tenderly makes it possible for his people to come back home to him after judgment. That is vividly depicted in the opening chapter of the book of Hosea. As a warning against the people's sin and idolatry, God tells

---

2 The Hebrew language doesn't really have a way of saying "holier" or "holiest" so achieves the same effect by repetition.

Hosea to give his children stark symbolic names: "No Compassion" and "Not My People" (Hosea 1:6, 9, see footnotes). However, the prophet describes a day when everything will change:

Yet the number of the Israelites will be like the sand of the sea, which cannot be measured or counted. And in the place where they were told: You are not my people, they will be called: Sons of the living God. And the Judeans and the Israelites will be gathered together. They will appoint for themselves a single ruler and go up from the land. (Hosea 1:10-11)

In the Old Testament, it's clear that, on the one hand, God is the all-seeing, all-knowing, all-powerful God who sits on the ultimate throne. He is unassailable, unsurprisable, imperturbable. He cannot be outflanked or outrun. He makes no missteps and never needs to reconsider. The old word for this was "impassible"— meaning "without passions". God simply isn't like us, and suffers from none of our limitations. And yet, God also shows himself to be the tenderest father imaginable (Exodus 4:22). He loves, delights in, weeps over and even sings over his children (Zephaniah 3:17). He's a both/and God.

Most of what we read in the Old Testament about God is really a description of God the Father (although clearly, because Father, Son and Spirit share the same essence, what's true of the Father is generally true of the other Persons of the Trinity). When Jesus Christ appears, the nature of our both/and God comes into even sharper focus.

2. THE BOTH/AND SON

Repeatedly in the New Testament, we are reminded that Jesus Christ is both very different from us (he's God himself) and just like us (a proper, living, breathing human being). That's expressed in lots of different ways. For example:

The Word became flesh and dwelt among us. We observed his glory, the glory as the one and only Son from the Father, full of grace and truth. (John 1:14)

[Christ Jesus] who, existing in the form of God, did not consider equality with God as something to be exploited. Instead he emptied himself by assuming the form of a servant, taking on the likeness of humanity. And when he had come as a man, he humbled himself by becoming obedient to the point of death—even to death on a cross. (Philippians 2:6-8)

The Westminster Confession of Faith, a document drawn up by a large gathering of Reformed pastors and theologians in London in the 17th century, expresses the "both/and-ness" of Jesus' identity like this:

The Son of God, the second Person in the Trinity, being very and eternal God, of one substance, and equal with the Father, did, when the fullness of time was come, take upon him man's nature, with all the essential properties and common infirmities thereof; yet without sin: being conceived by the power of the Holy Ghost, in the womb of the Virgin Mary, of her substance. So that two whole, perfect, and distinct natures, the Godhead and the manhood, were inseparably joined together in one person, without conversion, composition, or confusion.

Which person is very God and very man, yet one Christ,
the only Mediator between God and man. (8.2)

In other words, it's a both/and thing—God *and* man—
and if we lose sight of that, we end up with all kinds
of problems.

The authors of the Westminster Confession were by
no means the first to grapple with this tension. The first
four centuries of the Christian church were dominated
by arguments (and heresies) which revolved around
this question of whether Jesus was *really* God and *really*
human. The answer is very definitely yes to both; and
only when we hold on to that, do we have the Jesus of
the Bible—a rescuer who is both powerful enough to save
us and properly qualified as one of us to take our place.

This really is good news for people like us. The fact
that Jesus is a real human being like us takes the fact
that our God gets us to a whole new level. In Christ, God
knows us *from the inside*. He knows what it's like to be
one of us. He can actually, truly represent us. But that's
not the whole story. The fact that Jesus was also fully
God explains how he can transcend our limitations,
could flawlessly carry out every detail of the plan that
he had devised with his Father, and since then has
acted as our great high priest, bringing us into the very
presence of his Father (Hebrews 4:14-16).

3. THE BOTH/AND SPIRIT
While the Spirit is the self-effacing member of the
Godhead, who constantly deflects our attention away
from himself to the Son in particular, this both/and-
ness applies to his work too.

For one thing, it's both instant and gradual: the Spirit instantly brings us to new life in Christ (in regeneration and justification) and then continues the gradual work of transformation (or sanctification).

Here's one way in which Paul expresses that first dynamic, in Romans 8:15:

For you did not receive a spirit of slavery to fall back into fear. Instead, you received the Spirit of adoption, by whom we cry out, "Abba, Father!"

When we become Christians, the Spirit comes and takes up residence in our lives, making us permanently part of God's family. The Spirit's work in opening our eyes to Jesus, bringing us to life and enabling us to trust in Jesus reaches its climax when we are adopted as God's heirs. (This is the point of the gendered term "sons"—in the ancient world, daughters generally didn't inherit, so to elevate all of us together to the status of sons is actually a gloriously equalising thing). Knowing that the Spirit has moved in like this and permanently changed our relationship with God is a deeply freeing and ennobling thing.

But there's more: the Spirit who brings us into God's family *also* enables us to live in a way that increasingly aligns with that identity. Paul explains it like this:

I say, then, walk by the Spirit and you will certainly not carry out the desire of the flesh ... But the fruit of the Spirit is love, joy, peace, patience, kindness, goodness, faithfulness, gentleness, and self-control ... If we live by the Spirit, let us also keep in step with the Spirit. (Galatians 5:16, 22-23, 25)

The Spirit hasn't just united us to Christ and then left us to it. Every day, he also reassures, emboldens and galvanises us, growing his good fruit in us. His work is a both/and work.

A Both/And Salvation

Given all that we have seen of our both/and God, it isn't really a surprise to see that our salvation is a both/and thing too. And once we understand that, I think that it takes the sting out of some of the trickiest questions that we face. We'll look quickly at three examples.

1. BOTH ELECTION AND HUMAN RESPONSIBILITY

Salvation is a matter both of God's initiative and our response. Granted, this is a tricky and contentious area—but if we take the Bible seriously, it is impossible to avoid the conclusion that we owe our salvation to God:

For he chose us in him, before the foundation of the world, to be holy and blameless in love before him. He predestined us to be adopted as sons through Jesus Christ for himself, according to the good pleasure of his will, to the praise of his glorious grace that he lavished on us in the Beloved One. (Ephesians 1:4-6)

As Paul says at the start of Ephesians 2, we used to be "dead in ... trespasses", but God intervened. He brought us to life through the Spirit and made us his children. Our salvation is down to him. He chose us, brought us to new life and walks with us. But we still need to respond. Paul underlines this when he says that "you are saved by grace *through* faith" (v 8). Faith in the New Testament is a deliberate decision to trust God when he says that he has done everything it takes for us to be accepted, forgiven and transformed in Christ.

Are we chosen by God? Absolutely. Do we need to decide to follow him? Absolutely. It's a both/and thing.

2. BOTH GRACE AND WORKS

The same tension comes into view when we think about what it means for us to live as part of the family of God. We know that we are *saved* by grace alone (although we do have to respond), but what happens next? When it comes to living to please our Father, is it now all down to us? Is this where our effort kicks in? Or can we settle down and relax while we wait for heaven, secure in the fact that God has already done all the hard work? The reality is that this is another both/and thing!

The apostle Paul actually goes on to deal with these questions right after the headline statement we've just looked at:

> *For you are saved by grace through faith, and this is not from yourselves; it is God's gift—not from works, so that no one can boast. **For we are his workmanship, created in Christ Jesus for good works, which God prepared in advance for us to do.** (Ephesians 2:8-10)*

Are we saved by grace? Oh yes. Do we then need to put in effort? Oh yes. Paul makes it clear that salvation is by grace from beginning to end. But he also insists that both in coming to know Jesus and in pressing on with him, we have our part to play. In this case, we have to do the things he has made us for and rescued us for, in the strength that he has provided. We are both saved by grace and saved to do good works. As Paul says in Galatians, "For in Christ Jesus neither circumcision nor uncircumcision accomplishes anything; what matters is *faith working through love*" (Galatians 5:6).

This is exactly what the rest of the New Testament says too—even the book of James, which is sometimes thought of as being in opposition to Paul. James is writing to Christians who seem to have misunderstood the fact that Jesus calls us to the beautiful life of the kingdom—a life which is even richer and fuller than that sketched out in the Torah (see, for example, Matthew 5:17-20 in Jesus' Sermon on the Mount). James's readers think that they can trust Jesus and live however they like, and so he writes:

> *You see that a person is justified by works and not by faith alone. (James 2:24)*

That one sentence has caused all manner of havoc in the church down through the centuries. But, in a way, it's all been a bit unnecessary. James's concern is with the quality of faith. He's asking the question, *Is your faith the real thing?* That's plain when he writes in verse 17, "In the same way faith, if it does not have works, is dead by itself". In other words, without works, it isn't the real thing. Yes, it's trusting Jesus (faith) which saves us—but if it's the real deal, then it will flow into actions which please him. It's a both/and thing—which, reassuringly, is exactly what Paul said. The New

Testament is gloriously consistent. Salvation is a both/ and thing.

This means that being a Christian is neither a matter of sitting back smugly and waiting for heaven nor of anxiously working our religious socks off to make sure that we have done enough to please our Father. We can rest in the fact that we are his, saved by grace through faith, and then we can happily throw ourselves into serving him while we have breath, in the strength that he gives us.

3. BOTH NOW AND NOT YET

It is worth mentioning briefly one more way in which this plays out—in the New Testament, the kingdom of God is a both/and thing.

From the moment that Jesus launches his ministry with the words "The time is fulfilled, and the kingdom of God has come near. Repent and believe the good news" (Mark 1:15), everything changes. For generations, God's people had been waiting for him to intervene and set his King over his people, establishing a new kingdom. The arrival of Jesus meant that the moment had arrived—the King had come—and the ultimate mission of establishing an eternal kingdom in a renewed cosmos which endures forever is now under way. This means that what is happening in your church and mine right now has enduring, even eternal, significance! God's kingdom is being built hour by hour, day by day, week by week, in the stuff that we're doing for Jesus, and it will endure. It's his work, and he has guaranteed it. That's true even when things are going wrong or people are leaving your church or Satan is sowing division.

It also means that, as individuals, we can get out of bed in the morning and fall into bed at the end of the day knowing that we have eternal life—life with God, which starts now and will go on for ever (John 10:10). We can be confident that even when we can't see how, the details of our lives are all somehow swept up in God's plan and the glimpses of joy which we get now are just the beginning.

But of course our lives are a work in progress. And so are our churches. The kingdom of God is both now and not yet. And the "not yet" part means that, even in church, things are often a bit of a mess. Paul warns Timothy of what he can expect in his local church in Ephesus:

> But know this: Hard times will come in the last days.
> For people will be lovers of self, lovers of money,
> boastful, proud, demeaning, disobedient to parents,
> ungrateful, unholy, unloving, irreconcilable, slanderers,
> without self-control, brutal, without love for what is
> good, traitors, reckless, conceited, lovers of pleasure
> rather than lovers of God, holding to the form of
> godliness but denying its power. (2 Timothy 3:1-5)

It is pretty striking that a large chunk of the New Testament is taken up with letters dealing with major problems in church! Much of the rest is addressing how to cope when you come under pressure from society to give up on Jesus or at least to tone down your commitment. We all know that we live in a world where people (whether Christians or not) let each other down, act selfishly and don't live as they should. But remember, it won't always be like this.

A day is coming when the tension will finally be resolved—a day painted for us in Revelation:

The seventh angel blew his trumpet, and there were loud voices in heaven, saying, The kingdom of the world has become the kingdom of our Lord and of his Christ, and he will reign for ever and ever.

(Revelation 11:15)

But until then? When we grasp the fact that God has broken into our lives and our world and made a difference, it lifts our eyes to see that we're not just gritting our teeth and waiting for heaven! We have been made alive in Christ, and we get to taste and see that God is good right now. It also helps us to live with the frustrations and inconsistencies of life with people like ourselves in church, for we're not finished yet—but one day we will be, and in the words of the apostle John, "we will be like him because we will see him as he is" (1 John 3:2). The kingdom is both now and not yet.

It All Starts Here

The kind of life which this book describes and encourages isn't simply plucked out of the air, nor is it even simply the result of extracting helpful statements from across the Bible. It has deep roots in the nature of God and what it means to be his people. It all starts here. Every piece of reflection, every call to repentance, every encouragement to live differently begins here, in the nature and character of our God and the life to which he has called us—and for which he equips us—in the Lord Jesus Christ.

Mirror, Mirror, on the Wall (Why "Double Vision" is So Important)

The real danger of a book like this is that reading it can become a thoroughly depressing experience. Let's face it—we all know we could be more like Jesus, and having it pointed out isn't necessarily all that helpful. It can be demotivating and very, very guilt inducing.

But it turns out that this is another area where we need to make sure we are doing two things at once. The health of our Christian life depends on both remembering who we are in Christ (Spirit-created, indwelt and empowered people who are already like Jesus in lots of ways) and seeing the ways in which we continue to live in ways which don't fit with who we are (because of our sinful muscle memory and unruly desires). We need to look in the mirror and see both of these things at the same time.

This idea of *looking in the mirror* of God's word isn't an original one. Here's what James writes:

But be doers of the word and not hearers only, deceiving yourselves. Because if anyone is a hearer of the word and not a doer, he is like someone looking at his own face in a mirror. For he looks at himself, goes away, and immediately forgets what kind of person he was. But the one who looks intently into the perfect law of freedom and perseveres in it, and is not a forgetful hearer but a doer who works—this person will be blessed in what he does. (James 1:22-25)

Sometimes I think we read this more negatively than James intends. Yes, looking in the mirror of God's word clearly exposes us, but the nett result is blessing—seeing our freedom in Christ! It's a positive thing.

That's why at the end of each chapter, I've included these "mirror" sections. You'll find the first one over the page. They are here to help us to reflect on the issues raised in the chapter. But even that needs to be a both/and thing—one where we take hold of who we are in Christ, even as we face up to ways in which our lives don't fit with our new identity as children of God.

And one more thing... The whole Bible makes it pretty clear that "I'm not the final word on me". We each need the perspectives of those around us who know and love us. That's why I suggest that you ask someone (or a couple of people) who knows you well to give you a second opinion on your assessment of your strengths and weaknesses.

How do I think of the gospel?

1 is "I struggle to remember this", and 5 is "I am deeply aware of this".

Our Father is transcendent and glorious ////////

5   4   3   2   1

Jesus is fully God (and unlike me) //////////////

5   4   3   2   1

The Spirit has brought me to life //////////////

5   4   3   2   1

Salvation is God's initiative ///////////////////

5   4   3   2   1

We are saved by grace ///////////////////////

5   4   3   2   1

God's kingdom is being built now ////////////

5   4   3   2   1

Write down any categories where you have circled 3 or lower:

Can you think of specific reasons why any of these numbers might be low?

\\\\\\\\\\\\ **Our Father is immanent and gracious**

1   2   3   4   5

\\\\\\ **Jesus is fully human (and gets what it's like)**

1   2   3   4   5

\\\\\\\\\\\\\ **The Spirit is continually renewing me**

1   2   3   4   5

\\\\\\\\\\ **Humans are responsible for their decision**

1   2   3   4   5

\\\\\\\\\\\\\\\\ **We are saved to do good works**

1   2   3   4   5

\\\\\\\\\\\\\\\ **God's kingdom is not yet fulfilled**

1   2   3   4   5

Write down any areas that you think you need to address with the gospel:

CHAPTER 2

Both/And Identity

Are You an EISNTFPJ Too?

Personality tests are endlessly fascinating. You answer a few questions, and then the test tells you whether you're the life and soul of the party, or a caring, consensus-seeking relationship-builder. These tests promise to unlock the secrets of how we tick and to make it much easier for you to understand yourself and other people. Unfortunately, in my case, I'm always labelled as some variation of the "power-crazed dictator for life" and informed that I share a personality type with the likes of Genghis Khan (much to the amusement of my family or my co-workers!).

However, there are also some real dangers with these fun (if pseudoscientific) tests. For one thing, classifying us into one of a dozen or so categories can have the effect of making us think as if we are victims of our genetic make-up and/or upbringing and so locked into particular ways of thinking or acting—it can undermine any possibility that we (or other people) can change and grow. Equally, it can give us licence to justify doing what comes naturally to us. It's as if the introverts can all happily withdraw from people, while the extroverts blithely inflict their exuberance on everyone—all without any real need for anyone to think about the other because "it's just the way I am". The problem is that neither of these ways of thinking are very Christ-like.

The great news is of the gospel is that the Lord Jesus both sets us free and brings real, lifelong, deep-rooted change. We're not defined by a collection of letters or a one-word descriptor. Our natural personalities are rich and varied, and although there are ways of being and doing that come more naturally to each of us, the Spirit opens up all sorts of new ways in which to grow and change. In Christ, we are now both/and people, and that really does transform everything.

The Gospels present Jesus as a man who beautifully embodies both self-awareness and awareness of others: a man who is both completely happy in his own skin and yet never selfish or self-indulgent, even for an instant. Jesus is "full of [both] grace and truth" (John 1:14). He has all authority and yet is "lowly and humble" (Matthew 11:29). Jesus lives the both/and life; he is the real deal—courageous, tender, sensitive, confrontational, selfless, vulnerable, sensible, vibrant and awe-inspiring, all at the same time. No wonder Jesus himself is the single most attractive thing about Christianity!

If we're going to have any chance of living this kind of Jesus-shaped, both/and life, we're going to have to fight for it. But the great news is that in the Lord Jesus himself, God has already provided us with the resources we need to win. The first skirmish in the battle to live a joined-up both/and life takes place in our own hearts and minds. It starts with having a gospel-shaped, both/and identity. And what does that look like? It shows up in at least five ways.

1. WE ARE BOTH RIGHTEOUS AND SINFUL

You may not know much (or any!) Latin, but there is one phrase that it's worth getting to grips with: *simul iustus et peccator* ("righteous and sinner at the same time"). The phrase was coined by the Catholic monk turned radical Reformer Martin Luther in the 16th century to capture the fact that when we become Christians, we are both decisively, completely and permanently forgiven and yet (as every Christian has to admit) we still make all kinds of sinful choices. This is who we are: both righteous and sinful.

On the one hand, we have been justified by grace through faith. God has completely acquitted us of all wrongdoing and has replaced our terrible record with Jesus' own beautifully flawless version. Our debt has been paid, our guilt has been removed and our relationship with God has been restored. When we wake up every morning, we could not possibly be more secure.

But on the other hand, mentioning mornings may be more than enough to remind us that we are still very sinful. Self-preoccupation, grumpiness, harshness, laziness... You get the picture. Our lived experience makes it clear to us (and very definitely to the people we live and work with) that we have not yet reached a state of sinless perfection. Luther writes, "These two things are quite contrary ... that a Christian is righteous and beloved of God, and yet notwithstanding, he is a sinner".[3]

The challenge we face is to remember and live in the light of both of these truths at the same time.

The righteousness given to us in the gospel should (and does) produce a deep sense of security and confidence. We are loved and accepted by God. That, in itself, is more than enough to free us from all kinds of hang-ups and neuroses. Christians have *no need* to feel insecure. Remembering who we are in Christ should make a real-time difference in all that we do and grow in us a relaxed, trust-saturated confidence in the one who has already given us everything we need for life and godliness, and who will never, ever let us go. We don't need to prove ourselves or do anything to earn God's love.

But that isn't all we need to believe. The trouble with this kind of confidence is that, on its own, it can have an unfortunate tendency to quickly slide into arrogance—we'll start telling other people how it really is or what they really need to do, as if we have suddenly become experts, or we'll look down on them as though we have got everything together. This is why our confidence needs to be matched with an awareness of our own persisting sinfulness.

---

3 See Luther's *Commentary on Galatians* (1535) (James Clarke, 1953), p. 228.

Of course, if our own enduring sinfulness is *all* we cling on to, and becomes our preoccupation, that too will have all manner of damaging effects. It can very easily lead to excessive negativity and a shortfall in joy. Perhaps we'll feel paralysed by our guilt or shame, or we'll struggle to step out in serving other people because we feel we don't really have anything to offer. That's why we need to live out of the fact that we are both/and people!

Remembering that we're both righteous *and* sinners will produce something beautiful in us: true, self-forgetful humility. We're secure in Christ's righteousness. But we're still sinful. This simple but profound admission is the foundation of gentleness, generosity and gratitude.

2. WE ARE BOTH IMMORTAL AND MORTAL

It may seem almost too obvious to say, but sooner or later we are going to die. We are *mortal*. Just as with the Lord Jesus when he became human, the moment we are born as part of Adam's race, the clock starts ticking. It's only a matter of time before we die. None of us have an unlimited amount of time on earth. Even if we live to a ripe old age, sooner or later our time is up, and we die. And of course, we need to live in a way which reflects this.

Throughout church history, this note has often been sounded. In the 18th century, the young American Jonathan Edwards wrote a series of resolutions which capture the impact of our mortality powerfully. Here's a selection:

5. *Resolved, never to lose one moment of time; but improve it [in] the most profitable way I possibly can.*

6. *Resolved, to live with all my might, while I do live.*

7. *Resolved, never to do anything which I should be afraid to do if it were the last hour of my life.*

52. *I frequently hear persons in old age say how they would live, if they were to live their lives over again: Resolved, that I will live just so as I can think I shall wish I had done, supposing I live to old age.*[4]

CT Studd, the founder of the mission agency WEC, used to put it more succinctly when he said:

Only one life, 'twill soon be past,
Only what's done for Christ will last.

It's getting much easier to slip into thinking we're going to live for ever. In Australia, where I live, the average life expectancy has risen steadily over the past few decades to 83.94 years. Neither of my grandfathers made it to their retirement age of 65—but for me, even in my mid 50s, the end of my life seems a long way off! So I just don't think about it. Instead, I think about planning our next holiday, what needs to be done to the house, accumulating enough money from which to live when I do eventually stop work, and making sure there is enough going on in my life to entertain me in the meantime.

---

4 desiringgod.org/articles/the-resolutions-of-jonathan-edwards (accessed 1 May 2024).

I suspect this is true for most of us. We fritter away our time. We put off important things to next year. We say that once we've bought a house/fixed up the house/the kids have left home, *then* we'll do it. We need to remember that the clock is ticking for all of us.

But that's not the whole story. For we aren't *just* mortal. Paul puts it very simply in 1 Corinthians 15:

For just as in Adam all die, so also in Christ all will be made alive. (1 Corinthians 15:22)

It is certain that we will die—but if we have been joined to Christ by faith, then it is just as certain that we will be *raised with him*. We are people with a secure future and a guaranteed destination. 83.94 years is not all that we've got.

At one level, this is not the most blinding insight in the book: we all die, and we will all be raised. But it is surprisingly difficult to hold on to both truths at the same time!

Some of us become far too preoccupied with, and even afraid of, the fact that we are mortal. We live in dread of our own impending demise. We exercise frantically, counting every step. We monitor our heart rate and blood pressure and calorie intake. We avoid possible carcinogens, trans-fats and microplastics—anything which might shorten our life expectancy by the smallest fraction. We wrap ourselves in cotton wool. We forget that if we are Christians, who have been indissolubly joined to Christ, then we are immortal!

But some of us go to the other extreme. We are reckless. We act like we have no need to rest or to pace ourselves or to take time off because *time is short* and Jesus' call is serious: "If anyone wants to follow after me, let him deny himself, take up his cross, and follow me" (Mark 8:34). At the same time, we forget the fact that we are limited *creatures*. If Jesus needed to rest (see, for example, 4:38) then why on earth wouldn't we? The fact of our mortality (expressed in our frailty and limitedness) means that we must exercise some *self-care* if we are to function well in the longterm.

So which are we to prioritise? Maximising our durability and long-term health or expending ourselves passionately in the work of the kingdom, being willing to "burn out for God"? Self-care or self-denial? Once more, the answer is yes. We must do both. We must remember both that we are human—*mortal* and frail creatures who cannot do everything—and that we are *immortal*—and so can live with a freedom and selfless abandon as we expend ourselves for the sake of others.

I have to admit that it is particularly tricky to work out what healthy self-denying self-care looks like today. There is clearly a kind of self-denial that can lead to all kinds of psychological and physical damage in the longterm. But it's also clear that much of our contemporary language around self-care has the potential to spill over into selfishness and owes much more to the spirit of our age than Scripture. So what are we to do? A helpful way forward might be to ask ourselves two questions regularly:

1. Is there anything in my week which I don't really want to do, but I do it because it's of eternal value?

2. Is there anything in my week (or deliberately absent from my week) which reminds me that I am a frail human being who cannot do everything?

If the answer to either of these questions is no, we really should rethink.

3. WE ARE BOTH SIGNIFICANT AND INSIGNIFICANT

It follows naturally from this that, as people who are both mortal and immortal, we are also both significant and insignificant.

It is one of the most stunning revelations of the Bible that we are known by the God of the universe. He cares for us individually and, even more than that, pays careful attention to the smallest detail of our lives. Jesus himself makes this clear:

> *Aren't five sparrows sold for two pennies? Yet not one of them is forgotten in God's sight. Indeed, the hairs of your head are all counted. Don't be afraid; you are worth more than many sparrows. (Luke 12:6-7)*

> *Therefore I tell you: Don't worry about your life, what you will eat or what you will drink; or about your body, what you will wear. Isn't life more than food and the body more than clothing? Consider the birds of the sky: They don't sow or reap or gather into barns, yet your heavenly Father feeds them. Aren't you worth more than they? (Matthew 6:25-26)*

The gospel reassures us that we are personally significant—in fact, more than that, we are precious to God. How we all need to know that!

Every time I think of the fact that there are almost eight billion people in the world (and rising), it makes me feel very small. Insignificant even. Looking out over the city I live in, with its two million people, has the same effect. Gazing up at the brilliant southern-hemisphere night sky does it too. Which makes it all the more remarkable that the God of the cosmos knows my name. He calls me "son". As the author CS Lewis once said, "There are no ordinary people. You have never talked to a mere mortal."[5] The one who created all people has invited me to be part of his family and has promised me that I will know him for ever. Because of this, we are eternally, unimaginably significant, and we need to take hold of that.

But even as we grasp that, we need to remember something else—in the grand scheme of things, we are pretty insignificant!

For example, even as Psalm 103 affirms our inherent significance, it is quick to remind us of our cosmic insignificance:

As a father has compassion on his children,
so the LORD has compassion on those who fear him.
For he knows what we are made of,
remembering that we are dust.
As for man, his days are like grass—
he blooms like a flower of the field;
when the wind passes over it, it vanishes,
and its place is no longer known. (v 13-16)

The stark truth is that very few of us are remembered

---

5 CS Lewis, *The Weight of Glory* (HarperOne, 2001), p. 45.

for long or far beyond the immediate circle of our families and our closest friends. That means that arrogantly acting as if we are God's gift to humanity (or even just his gift to those who know us) is extremely foolish. Speaking as if the entire work of the kingdom of God depends on us or as if we are irreplaceable, able to do things in a way which no one else can, is never a good idea. Remembering our insignificance in the grand scheme of things is a key step to the humility which Christ calls us to.

This too then is an area in which we must hold on to paradoxical truths at the same time.

In his kindness, God has assured us that we are precious to him, which lifts our heads high. We cannot afford to let go of that. And yet, in the same breath, he reminds us that he is God and we are not, to keep us humble. This is how we must see ourselves. And this spills over into one more aspect of our self-understanding.

4. WE ARE BOTH COMPLETE IN CHRIST AND WORKS IN PROGRESS

As followers of Jesus, we often flit between anxious self-doubt on the one hand (feeling that we are so far short of where we should be) and complacency on the other (feeling that because Jesus has already done all it takes to rescue us, we don't really need to fret about growing in godliness). In truth, we need to make sure that we find our security in who we are in Christ while also remembering that we are never more than works in progress.

The apostle John draws these two threads together beautifully in his first letter. He starts by saying:

See what great love the Father has given us that we should be called God's children—and we are! ... Dear friends, we are God's children now. (1 John 3:1-2)

Right now, there are a whole host of things that can be said of us which underline the fact that because of God's grace to us in Christ, a decisive, permanent change has come upon us. So, for example, in this very moment...

- I am a child (and heir) of God (e.g. 1 John 3:1).

- I have been forgiven on the basis of Jesus' death and resurrection (e.g. Romans 8:1).

- I am a new creation in Christ (e.g. 2 Corinthians 5:17).

- I have been reconciled to God in Christ (e.g. v 18).

- I have been born of God by the Spirit (e.g. 1 John 5:1).

- I have been united to Christ by faith (e.g. Romans 6:10-11).

- I share in the eternal love of the Father, Son and Spirit (e.g. John 14:21).

In Christ, you are complete; you don't need to add any achievements or tick off anything from your to-do list or attain a particular standard of love and morality in order to make those statements true of you. They already are.

But John isn't finished—even as we live out of our identity as those whom God has decisively changed, we are to keep pressing on as God continues his work of transformation in us:

*Dear friends, we are God's children now, and **what we will be has not yet been revealed**. We know that when he appears, we will be like him because we will see him as he is. (1 John 3:2)*

We need to remember that none of us is the finished article. None of us is perfectly Christ-like. We need to press on, being "transformed by the renewing of [our] mind" (Romans 12:2). John expresses it like this:

And everyone who has this hope in him purifies himself just as he [Christ] is pure. (1 John 3:3)

Is there an area of your life or character where you have quietly given up the fight against sin? Or perhaps silently told yourself that "I have got that sorted—this is no longer a problem for me"? You may even have thanked God that you are now a "mature" Christian and so can relax. If that's you, I'd recommend that you stop here and read Luke 18:9-14! The reality is that none of us is the finished article.

Knowing who we are in Christ, and who we will be, and that God is in the process of changing us is the way to both humility and growth.

Knowing God, Knowing Me

At the start of his magnum opus, *The Institutes of the Christian Religion*, the Reformer John Calvin pointed out that "all true wisdom consists of two parts—the knowledge of God and the knowledge of ourselves".[6] Often it is the latter that we fall down on (and do so spectacularly). But if we grasp this both/and identity, it will have a profound effect on the way in which we see ourselves—from the moment we get up in the morning to the moment we collapse into bed at night. On the one hand, we will be essentially secure and positive, and a joy to be around, as one who is grounded in their identity in Christ. But on the other, we won't be obnoxious, claiming that we are always right, constantly justifying our actions or insisting that we have pure motives and great intentions.

Our basic self-understanding will line up with this famous statement from John Newton, a slave trader who was seized by the grace of God and went on to be a minister:

> I am not what I ought to be—ah, how imperfect and deficient! I am not what I wish to be—I abhor what is evil, and I would cleave to what is good! I am not what I hope to be—soon, soon shall I put off mortality, and with mortality all sin and imperfection. Yet, though I am not what I ought to be, nor what I wish to be, nor what I hope to be, I can truly say, I am not what I once was; a slave to sin and Satan; and I can heartily join with the apostle, and acknowledge, "By the grace of God I am what I am."[7]

---

6 John Calvin, *The Institutes of the Christian Religion*, Book 1 1.1.

7 John Newton, *The Christian Spectator*, vol. 3 (1821), p186.

How do I think of myself?

1 is "rarely", and 5 is "constantly".

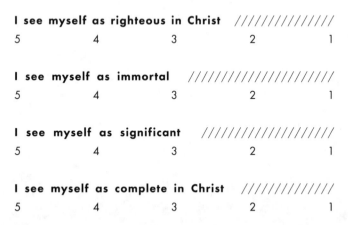

I see myself as righteous in Christ ///////////////
5   4   3   2   1

I see myself as immortal /////////////////////
5   4   3   2   1

I see myself as significant ////////////////////
5   4   3   2   1

I see myself as complete in Christ /////////////
5   4   3   2   1

Write down any categories where you have circled 3 or lower:

Can you think of specific reasons why any of these numbers might be low?

\\\\\\\\\\\\\\\\\\\\\\\\\\\\\\\\ **I see myself as sinful**

1   2   3   4   5

\\\\\\\\\\\\\\\\\\\\\\\\\\\\\\ **I see myself as mortal**

1   2   3   4   5

\\\\\\\\\\\\\\\\\\\\\\\\\ **I see myself as insignificant**

1   2   3   4   5

\\\\\\\\\\\\\\\\\\\\ **I see myself as a work in progress**

1   2   3   4   5

Write down any areas that you think you need to address with the gospel:

CHAPTER 3

Both/And Relationships

A Rock and a Hard Place

Imagine for a moment: Christmas is coming, and the annual exchange of messages negotiating how and when your extended family will celebrate has just kicked off. Your sister assumes (as always) that everyone will come to her. Your brother clearly wants to stay at home. Your mum says she just wants everyone to be happy, but you know she'll secretly be heartbroken if all the grandchildren aren't there and at the centre.

So what should you do? Allow your siblings to be selfish or stand up to them and cause a family row? Be considerate of their needs or act in the best interests of your part of the family? Bend or demand? It's complicated, isn't it?

Church family doesn't tend to be any simpler! Whether we're dealing with family, church members or our friends and neighbours, relationships are complicated, even when we are followers of the Lord Jesus. If anything, being a Christian makes relationships even trickier!

Once we have grasped the both/and nature of the gospel and understood that this changes the way we think about ourselves, we soon realise that it should reshape the way in which we treat other people too. Both/and will be the bifocal lens through which we look at the world. When we're interacting with others, we will be both optimistic and pessimistic, both generous and realistic. We'll recognise that we live in a world (and serve in a church) full of both/and people, and we'll relate to them in a both/and way.

Not surprisingly, this is exactly what Jesus did and what he encouraged us to do as his followers. But this can be pretty complicated to negotiate in practice. We see that in what Jesus says to his disciples in Matthew 10 about dealing with those "wolves" who oppose them:

> Look, I'm sending you out like sheep among wolves.
> Therefore be as **shrewd as snakes** and as **innocent as doves**. (v 16)

On the one hand, we need to take seriously the reality of life in a broken world. Naivety is not the same thing as godliness. As Jesus said elsewhere, "The children of this age are more shrewd than the children of light in dealing with their own people" (Luke 16:8). Being naïve and gullible is clearly *not* a good thing. We need to be realistic about mixed motives, pretence, manipulation and a hundred other manifestations of sin in our messed-up world.

On the other hand, being cynical isn't a godly option either. We need to make sure that we don't slip into thinking that sin has eradicated every last vestige of the goodness of God, displayed in both his creatures and the rest of creation. It's important to hold on to the glorious positivity which flows from the fact that our God is in the transformation business; he brings the dead to life and will one day bring all his work to completion in a stunning new creation in which Christ himself will stand powerfully at the centre.

Even when we're dealing with "wolves", relating to people in a Christ-like way is complicated—and this really is only the beginning.

The "Problem" with Jesus

Before we go any further, we do need to flag up a bit of a problem. This book is all about "living and leading like Jesus" because that's exactly what God asks of us and equips us to do. That's why Paul tells the Corinthians to "imitate me, as I also imitate Christ" (1 Corinthians 11:1). It's why John says, "The one who says he remains in him should walk just as he walked" (1 John 2:6). Because Jesus is 100% human, it is perfectly reasonable for us to model ourselves on him.

But we do need to remember that while Jesus really is a human being like us, he is the one perfect, flawless, sinless human being (unlike us, in case you were in any doubt!).

That means that when it comes to relating to people, Jesus is our model and example. But we need to face the fact that (even with the Spirit's help), we'll never manage to relate *exactly* like him until the new creation. We don't have his insight or his wisdom, his tenderness or his resilience. And the fact is that we are messed up in a way that Jesus isn't. All of us have been shaped and scarred by sin. All of us struggle against the flesh. But we know that in our failures, Jesus relates to us with the same insight, wisdom and tenderness that we are seeking to show to others. He is gracious.

Our Default Settings

There's another factor to consider too. How we relate to other people is complicated not only by the way in which we've been shaped and scarred by sin but also by a whole range of other factors which may not be sinful but which, nonetheless, run very deep: things like our family of origin and our cultural background.

For example, I am a Northern Irish male who grew up in a Presbyterian family in the midst of "the Troubles"—a violent political conflict which gripped this small community for 30 years from the late 1960s. I was educated at an academically selective grammar school (which was basically a government-funded school that felt and acted like a private school), and I went on to study at university.

All those things have had an influence on the way in which I relate to other people. For instance, I have a strong sense of responsibility and the importance of treating everyone the same. I value hard work and expect everyone else to work hard too. I have a penchant for attempting to lighten serious moments with humour. I also sometimes struggle with empathy and am not the best at expressing my care for people in words. I know I can also make people feel guilty and even condemned if they are not as disciplined as I (usually) am. I tend to get caught up in what I'm doing and ignore what's going on around me.

Some of these are good and helpful instincts, and some of them are not, and in a whole load of cases, it will depend on the situation. But the point is that these are my default settings. If I just freewheel, then this is how I will relate to others. The problem is that the Bible makes it clear that freewheeling is not okay for sinful people like you and me. We're called to follow Jesus, our example, in the ways in which we relate—and there is nothing to suggest that Jesus just went with the flow of what was expected of him by his culture or his family. In fact, he often did the opposite (Mark 3:31-35; John 4:7-9, 27). Jesus consistently loved God and loved other people.

The challenge, then, that we all face is making sure that the way in which we relate to other people is shaped by the gospel itself. That's the case both in our relationships with those who don't know Jesus yet and with our brothers and sisters in our church family (which is the focus of the rest of this chapter).

We are called to commit ourselves to both/and relationships. What does that look like? I'd suggest that it involves at least five things.

1. BOTH GIVING AND RECEIVING

Our starting point must be owning the fact that we both need other people and are needed by other people. At the end of this book, we'll spend a whole chapter looking at this (because we are called to live for Jesus *as the church* and not simply in isolation as individuals), but it's worth flagging up now because this principle needs to be worked out in every single relationship. We are never simply either givers or takers. We are called to give and to receive.

If you want a quick test to see which way you instinctively lean, think about this: you have been out for a meal with friends, and it's time to pay the bill. Do you sneak up and settle it before they have a chance? Or how do you feel if you discover that they have beaten you to it? Perhaps you agree up front that you are splitting it, so no one has to deal with this issue!

Most healthy relationships don't run one way. Even in the Gospels, where the focus is clearly on what Jesus does for us and gives to us, there are moments when he is delighted to receive from others (for example, the unnamed woman who anoints his feet in Luke 7:36-50). The truth is that as Christians we are those who need constantly to both receive and give. And one of the ways we do that is by...

2. BOTH SPEAKING AND LISTENING

Our basic responsibility to our brothers and sisters is to remind one another of the gospel, building each other up as we speak "the truth in love". The apostle Paul expresses it like this in Ephesians 4:

> But **speaking the truth in love**, let us grow in every
> way into him who is the head—Christ. From him
> the whole body, fitted and knit together by every
> supporting ligament, promotes the growth of the body
> for building itself up in love by the proper working of

each individual part ... Therefore, putting away lying,
speak the truth, *each one to his neighbour, because we*
are members of one another. (Ephesians 4:15-16, 25)

This truth-speaking isn't simply avoiding lying to each other—although, as verse 25 shows, it certainly includes that. Speaking "the truth in love" means speaking the full gamut of the gospel, as we remind, apply, exhort and comfort one another with what God has done, is doing and will do for us in the Lord Jesus Christ.

That's why it's so important that Christians gather week by week to *meet together*. A key part of those gatherings is clearly engaging with God himself. (The Bible puts the emphasis on hearing God speak through Scripture and then responding to him as we sing, pray and share the Lord's Supper together, for example.) But alongside this "vertical" dimension, gathering as God's people is also supposed to be a "horizontal" or relational event.

If we're honest, sometimes we make what we do on Sundays "all about me"—we come to hear a sermon preached or to walk up to the front to receive a piece of bread and a sip of wine, but even though we do those things in the presence of others, it's not really a shared experience. We don't actually *interact* with anyone else. Or if we do, we don't really say anything meaningful to them.

In most Australian churches, there is an almost sacred commitment to having morning tea after the service. This is neither restricted to tea (in fact, the quality of the coffee served is often a source of contention) nor even to liquids—a good morning tea includes an impressive range of both sweet and savoury delicacies and preferably an expansive range of cut fruit as well. But often, the conversation doesn't match the quality of the food. Most of us struggle to escape banalities and, in particular, to speak about the joys and struggles of serving Jesus. But struggle we must for it is our responsibility to take every opportunity to speak to our brothers and sisters about the things that matter most.

So every Sunday, before I go to meet with my church family, I try to ask God to help me to actively listen to others and seek out opportunities to encourage them in the gospel, as we speak together about Jesus.

For some of us, it's the speaking that's hard, and this is where we must start. Or perhaps, like me, you're someone who loves to talk. You were like that from your earliest days. Some of us come from cultures (or a whole island in my case) that are known for talking. For those of us who work in ministry roles, we have in most cases been trained to talk, perhaps even studying for years to improve the quality of what we say and how we say it. Talking is not the hard bit for us.

You only have to put me in a Bible-study group for a vivid example of how this plays out. I usually go in with both my own prayers and my wife's encouragement ringing in my ears: "I must not talk too much!" Usually I start off reasonably well until, at some point, there is an unanswered question left hanging in the air... And it's just too much to resist. I talk. I preach. I teach. On a bad night, you could even say I lecture!

The trouble is that the same scene is replayed in almost every relationship I have. Talking is my sweet spot. Listening? Not so much. But it really, really matters that I do it. Why? Because I really need other people to speak the truth into my life.

One of the specific dangers of being in leadership in church or in a teaching role (or, to be honest, simply being around church for a long time), is that we start thinking of ourselves solely as givers and not receivers; as talkers and not listeners. I once had a conversation with a well-known pastor at a conference who said that it was the first time he had come to an event that he hadn't been speaking at for over 20 years. I found that quite frightening because the gospel shape of relationships demands that we care enough about others to speak the gospel into their lives *and* that we know enough of our own need to be desperate for others to speak into our lives, whether we're usually up front or happily seated at the back!

If we're Christians, then our brothers and sisters have the right to do this. But sometimes, they do need to be invited. We need to work hard at having the kind of Christ-centred conversations which matter, and at making it easy for others to speak to us as we need it so that we are both built up.

3. BOTH POINTING OUT SIN AND OWNING OURS

This mutuality extends far beyond speaking. If speaking the truth in love is the foundation of our care for each other, then bearing one another's burdens is the main load-bearing wall.

The New Testament sets out our responsibility to do everything we can to support our brothers and sisters when they are going through tough times, and particularly *when it comes to sliding into sin*. Paul tackles this head on in his letter to the churches in Galatia:

Brothers and sisters, if someone is overtaken in any wrongdoing, you who are spiritual, restore such a person with a gentle spirit, watching out for yourselves so that you won't also be tempted. Carry one another's burdens; in this way you will fulfil the law of Christ.
(Galatians 6:1-2)

In a way, this is a natural extension of speaking the truth in love. If we see a member of our church family being "overtaken [by] wrongdoing", we cannot stand by. *It really is our problem.* We need to challenge their sin and speak the gospel to them with a view to restoring them—that is, enabling them to get back on track with following Jesus. This isn't an optional extra but a basic requirement of being united in Christ.

For some of us, this is a truly frightening prospect. It seems intrusive—arrogant, even. We would rather stick pins in our eyes than have conversations like this with our Christian family! But this is what God asks of us. We're to care enough for one another to have those hard conversations because we know that this is how we grow together in the gospel. We get an example of this earlier in the letter, in 2:11-14, where Paul describes how he stood up to Peter (here named Cephas), lovingly pointing out that he had lost the plot! The great thing is that this doesn't appear to have damaged their relationship but actually enhanced it (see 2 Peter 3:15-16). This is what it looks like to speak the truth in a costly way to brothers and sisters for their good.

There are, however, some of us for whom pointing out the sin of other people seems all too easy. When it comes to discerning ways in which other people fall short and pointing it out to them, we are ready and able to do whatever it takes! But the problem is that there is something else we need to do at the same time. Notice what Paul says at the end of Galatians 6:1. He adds, "... watching out for yourselves so that you won't also be tempted". One temptation will be to think of ourselves as superior—to apply the gospel to others without applying it to ourselves. Galatians 6 continues:

For if anyone considers himself to be something when he is nothing, he deceives himself. Let each person examine his own work, and then he can take pride in himself alone, and not compare himself with someone else. For each person will have to carry his own load.
(Galatians 6:3-5)

Paul is quick to point out that when the church family is working in a gospel-shaped way, both of these things happen simultaneously: we are owning our own sin, thinking hard about how we are relating to others, as well as keeping a loving eye on others. It is this both/and-ness which enables deep relationships to grow.

If we grasp the fact that we need other people, it will stop us from posing as experts, endlessly telling other people what *they* need to know. It will also stop us from thinking that "I'm the final word on *me*" and drive us to listen to other people's perspectives, even on our sin.

There is a beautiful balance here: at the end of the day, we are responsible for our own relationship with God but we are not disconnected from others—we have a shared responsibility to live together in repentance and faith. Once again, it's a "both/and" thing.

4. BOTH REALISING WE'RE THE SAME AND CELEBRATING OUR UNIQUENESS

If we are going to build and maintain rich relationships, then we need to have a profound understanding both of the fact that we are all made of the same stuff (or, if you prefer, of all that we have in common as humans) and that we are unique individuals.

On the one hand, we do need to understand "how people work" in general. There are some things that are true of all of us: there are some things which we never escape (like the fact that we are still sinful); there are some things that we are all prone to (like worshipping God substitutes, or idols); there are some things that we all aspire to (like security, significance and satisfaction); there are some things which we all have in common (we all eat, breathe, sleep, have parents, etc.). But there are other aspects of us which are uniquely "us". Our experiences, thought processes, influences, quirks and abilities are all different.

In 1 Corinthians 12, this is captured in a vivid extended metaphor:

For just as the body is one and has many parts, and all the parts of that body, though many, are one body—so also is Christ. For we were all baptised by one Spirit into one body—whether Jews or Greeks, whether

*slaves or free—and we were all given one Spirit to
drink. Indeed, the body is not one part but many.*
(1 Corinthians 12:12-14)

We are organically linked, as we have seen—we are part
of the same "body". But to state the obvious, not every
part of the body is identical or interchangeable.

*If the foot should say, "Because I'm not a hand, I don't
belong to the body", it is not for that reason any less a
part of the body. And if the ear should say, "Because
I'm not an eye, I don't belong to the body", it is not for
that reason any less a part of the body. If the whole
body were an eye, where would the hearing be? If the
whole body were an ear, where would the sense of smell
be? But as it is, God has arranged each one of the parts
in the body just as he wanted. And if they were all the
same part, where would the body be? As it is, there are
many parts, but one body. The eye cannot say to the
hand, "I don't need you!" Or again, the head can't say
to the feet, "I don't need you!" On the contrary, those
parts of the body that are weaker are indispensable.*
(v 15-22)

In other words, we're all different, and we all need each
other. But this isn't just about utility (valuing what
people can bring to the team). Paul says that every
part of the body, even those that appear weakest,
is indispensable and therefore must not simply be
tolerated but honoured:

*And those parts of the body that we consider less
honourable, we clothe these with greater honour,*

and our unrespectable parts are treated with greater respect, which our respectable parts do not need.

(v 23-24)

All this means that in our relationships, we need to remember that everyone else is *both* just like us *and* utterly unique.

It's not hard to see the dangers of forgetting what we have in common. If we see someone as fundamentally different to us and assume that we have nothing in common or nothing to offer each other, we probably won't even try to engage with them or build a relationship. Our attitude will quickly become an insurmountable barrier to real friendship or deep care. The great thing is that our shared humanity means that we can build relationships with *anyone* for the sake of the gospel—it's possible to forge friendships across differences because there is a fundamental similarity underneath.

It's also not hard to spot the dangers of assuming that everyone else is just like me. Sometimes, I slip into thinking that all sensible people everywhere think and act like I do. That can mean all kinds of things—from believing that lunch at 12.35pm is an immoveable feast to assuming that a short meeting is a good meeting and that anecdotes about sport are inherently engaging! More seriously, it can lead to assuming that if something isn't an issue for me, then it isn't an issue. This can show itself in all kinds of ways (when extroverts don't think about introverts, men don't think about women, engineers don't think about artists, locals don't think about immigrants or older people don't think about younger people—and, of course, vice versa).

Gospel-shaped relationships are really rich, really freeing and really tricky because they are built on remembering that the other person is both just like me and delightfully different.

5. BOTH SPEAKING STRAIGHT AND BEING TENDER

Over time, most parents perfect the "good cop, bad cop" routine, where one gets to play the sympathetic role and the other issues all kinds of apocalyptic threats. Whether this approach is effective is another matter— but I suspect that most of us fall more easily into one of those roles than the other. Generally, either softness or robustness comes more easily to us. Of course, this can play out differently in different relationships at different times; I only have to think of my relationship with my daughters to have multiple examples of how difficult it is to be consistent! But the point is that in every relationship, we can't choose between either toughness or tenderness, or it will lead to disaster. It's a both/and thing.

Perhaps the most compelling example of this is the way in which God himself treats his people, ancient Israel, in the Old Testament. We've already seen one striking example from Hosea. When Hosea has a child with his sexually promiscuous wife, Gomer, Yahweh gives specific instructions about the boy:

> *Name him Lo-ammi,*
> *for you are not my people,*
> *and I will not be your God.*
> *Yet the number of the Israelites*
> *will be like the sand of the sea,*

which cannot be measured or counted.
And in the place where they were told:
You are not my people,
they will be called: Sons of the living God.

(Hosea 1:9-10)

These words are both clearly tough and deeply compassionate. This is a feature which also constantly recurs in the ministry of Jesus. Jesus is blunt and confrontational *and* deeply tender, and he is so at the same time:

Jerusalem, Jerusalem, who kills the prophets and stones those who are sent to her. How often I wanted to gather your children together, as a hen gathers her chicks under her wings, but you were not willing! See, your house is left to you desolate. For I tell you, you will not see me again until you say, "Blessed is he who comes in the name of the Lord"! (Matthew 23:37-39)

The challenge for us is to maintain this same combination of courage and compassion, of candour and sensitivity, as we follow in the steps of the Lord Jesus—but boy, is that hard to pull off!

If we're honest, most of us will tend to favour one approach over the other. Either we'll tend to speak our mind without much thought for the consequences, or we'll be very slow to speak in case we cause damage. If we veer naturally towards toughness, the danger is that we are valuing our own integrity and "truth" in the abstract more than the people we are speaking to. If we rarely say a troubling word to anyone, the danger is that we are simply living to please other people and aren't actually loving them enough to care about their growth in godliness.

This is an area where we need to be honest with ourselves and ask for God's help to work against the grain of our personality and entrenched habits. If we think of ourselves as plain speakers, who call a spade a spade, then we probably need God to soften us and help us to speak tenderly to people. If we shy away from ever raising anything that might be vaguely awkward, then we need to ask God to toughen us up—because the way of Christ-likeness is to be both tough and tender at the same time.

So... What about Christmas?

So where are you going to spend Christmas this year? Thinking about the both/and-ness of relationships may not have resolved all the fraught issues around that. But hopefully it has exposed some of your default ways of relating to others and how that might be selling other people short (even those you know best). The great thing is that Jesus invites us to step with him into authentic relationships which are defined and driven by the gospel itself—and his Spirit stands ready to help us to change and grow.

How do I relate to other people?

1 is "I struggle", and 5 is "This comes naturally to me".

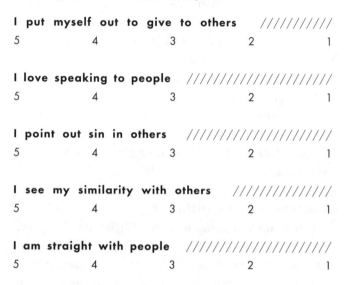

I put myself out to give to others ////////////
5   4   3   2   1

I love speaking to people ////////////////////
5   4   3   2   1

I point out sin in others ////////////////////
5   4   3   2   1

I see my similarity with others ///////////////
5   4   3   2   1

I am straight with people /////////////////////
5   4   3   2   1

Write down any categories where you have circled 3 or lower:

Can you think of specific reasons why any of these numbers might be low?

\\\\\\\\\\\\\\\\\ **I allow others to serve me**
1   2   3   4   5

\\\\\\\\\\\\\\\\\\\\\\\\\\ **I am a good listener**
1   2   3   4   5

\\\\\\\\\\\\\\\\\\\\\\\\\\\\\\\ **I own my own sin**
1   2   3   4   5

\\\\\\\\\\\\\\\\\\\\\ **I realise I am a one-off**
1   2   3   4   5

\\\\\\\\\\\\\\\\\\\\\ **I am tender with people**
1   2   3   4   5

Write down any areas that you think you need to address with the gospel:

CHAPTER 4

Both/And Ministry

This Chapter Is for You!

"Ministry" is one of those words which can be taken to mean pretty much what we want it to mean. Historically, it was the preserve of those who were "Ministers" with a capital "M"—almost always ordained, paid and male. But over the past few decades, more churches have woken up to the glorious biblical reality that if you are part of the body of Christ, you are (or really should be!) involved in ministry at some level.

Earlier I described ministry as "doing stuff at church". But, of course, ministry is a bit more than that. For a start, it's doing stuff *to the glory of God*. And if we are doing stuff to the glory of God, it must involve giving God the credit for what we do. This means that, at a basic level, all ministry is linked in some way to communicating the gospel.

It's also stating the obvious to say that not all ministries are alike—some ministries are absolutely crucial to the life of every local church (like the preaching of the word), whereas others are optional. (Not every church, for example, needs to have English conversation classes for internationals.) There are also some roles which only a few can do (like being an elder) and others where the only qualifications needed are a servant heart and the ability to bend over (like cleaning the toilets). I'll say a little more about all of that in the next chapter when we look at both/and leadership. But this chapter isn't really about what ministry is. It's about what goes on in our hearts and minds as soon as any of us start to do stuff in church. Whatever we do in church (or outside it, for that matter) should be done like Jesus. That's why this chapter isn't just for or about leaders— it's for anyone who ever does anything in church. This chapter is for all of us.

The tricky thing about ministry is remembering that while it's all about God (we serve for his glory and in his strength—he's the one who does the heavy lifting), we also need to be aware of what's going on in our heads and hearts. Whatever we do, we need to do it in a way which pleases the person we are doing it for. That plays out in a whole range of ways.

1. BOTH DEPENDENT ON GOD AND COMMITTED TO WORKING HARD

Some of us like to fix things. We do it instinctively. When we're presented with a problem or a challenge, we spring into action. We talk, we think, we plan, we act. We don't rest until the issue is solved. The problem with being wired this way is that it's very easy to slip into thinking that "we've got this covered!"—or that if we simply work harder / think longer / talk more, then everything will fall into place. It's as if we rely on God only to come through at the end and put the cherry on top of all our hard work! If we start thinking like this, praying will begin to seem like an unnecessary delay to getting the job done, and we'll start to see other people as obstacles to the success of our mission!

Clearly, that's not a great way to go about ministry.

Some of us, however, instinctively commit every problem to God. We habitually leave things with him (or possibly just to someone else). The trouble is that we may not actually get around to doing anything *ourselves*. We may start to embody the old cliché of being "so heavenly-minded that they are no earthly use"—much to the frustration of our friends in the previous paragraph.

It's not hard to see that this is another example of the need for both/and-ness in the Christian life. Nehemiah gives us a great example of being both dependent on God and willing to take action. When he had started to rebuild the wall of Jerusalem and became aware of those who were trying to frustrate his work, he said simply, "So we prayed to our God and stationed a guard because of them day and night" (Nehemiah 4:9).

All ministry has to start with the fact that it is God who does the real work. He is the only one who can open blind eyes, bring dead people to life and transform sinful people like us to be like the Lord Jesus. All this happens only through the Spirit as God works through his word.

The reality is that you are not the Holy Spirit, and nor am I! I have been involved in ministry for over 40 years, and I have never changed anyone. In fact, I've never even managed to change myself. It is God who does the heavy lifting. This is where ministry starts, continues and finishes. No matter how much experience we have, or how skilful we are, we will never get past this truth: it is God who does the real work, and he is the only one who deserves the credit.

But that doesn't mean we just sit back and do nothing. Paul captures this dynamic beautifully in 1 Corinthians:

> *I planted, Apollos watered, but God gave the growth. So, then, neither the one who plants nor the one who waters is anything, but only God who gives the growth. Now he who plants and he who waters are one, and each will receive his own reward according to his own labour. For we are God's co-workers. (3:6-9)*

God has given us the remarkable privilege of being his "co-workers". Like a dad allowing his three-year-old daughter to "help", God graciously enlists us in his great work: we get to plant and water the seeds of the gospel. We get to speak his living, powerful truth into people's lives. We get to care for people and persuade them and cheer them on and love them—and, let's face it, that can be pretty hard work—but only God produces growth. Remembering that paradox is what lies at the heart of all gospel ministry. And it sets the tone for everything we do.

2. BOTH CONFIDENT AND HUMBLE

What we believe about who is doing the real work can be seen in the way we go about things but also in how we *talk* about what we're doing. When we speak about church and what we're doing, the tone is always a real giveaway and often exposes issues with the way in which we are thinking.

Sometimes we talk up what we're doing with great confidence. "We *know* it's going to be a great time. We're *sure* God's going to use this to transform our community." I'm sure you recognise the vibe. Sometimes this is born of genuine enthusiasm and conviction, but at other times it sounds more like wishful thinking than anything else. At its worst, it can end up sounding boastful or even hubristic.

Conversely, we can end up sounding far too apologetic: "Only God can do this, and we're not going to be of much use to him. In fact, we'd be surprised if this makes any difference to anything at all." We're so worried about talking things up that we very effectively pour a bucket of cold water on anything that might actually be good! Or perhaps we're adept at talking in a way that makes us look humble—but, in reality, we're just disguising our pride with the kind of language that we know goes down well in church.

So what are we to do?

We need to recognise that confidence is good when it is confidence in God and what he has promised, and that humility is good when it flows from a recognition that we are weak but God is strong and has said he will use people like us for his glory.

As we've seen, one of the most striking things about the Lord Jesus is that he manages to be both supremely confident—happily facing down all-comers and never wavering for a moment from his mission—and deeply humble. There is not the faintest sniff of ego or self-promotion in the Gospels. And ministry for us should have the same shape and tone.

On the one hand, we should be able to say with Paul, "I am able to do all things through him who strengthens me" (Philippians 4:13). That's an astonishing statement! Paul clearly doesn't mean that he can leap between tall buildings or cure cancer simply by thinking about it. But he does mean that he is able to cope with anything that's thrown at him. He can live for Christ in every situation because of what God has already done for him and supplied to him. His confidence is rock solid. But that hasn't spilled over into arrogance.

So often for us, confidence means self-confidence. We slide into thinking that we are something special, or, at the very least, that "I've got this". But not Paul. His confidence was a beautifully humble confidence. But it hadn't come easily. This kind of humility had to be learned. In the verses before that epic statement of confidence, Paul wrote this:

> *I don't say this out of need, for I have learned to be content in whatever circumstances I find myself. I know how to make do with little, and I know how to make do with a lot. In any and all circumstances I have learned the secret of being content—whether well fed or hungry, whether in abundance or in need.*
> *(Philippians 4:11-12)*

His own experience of life (and suffering in particular) had taught Paul both that God can be trusted and that, on his own, he (Paul) couldn't be—which is why he was both confident and humble.

3. BOTH USING MY GIFTS AND READY TO DO ANYTHING

One of the challenges of ministry in the local church is working out what particular stuff I should do. Should I only do the things I love? The things that I think I'm good at? The things that I think matter? Should I just do what needs to be done, whatever it happens to be (and regardless of whether I'm any good at it)? Even if we find ourselves in a role such as "pastor" or "women's minister", it's still difficult to discern what tasks we should be doing ourselves and what we should leave or delegate to others.

One of the glorious realities of the church is that God has given us everything we need for our life together in each other. Paul captures this vividly in 1 Corinthians 12:

> *Now there are different gifts, but the same Spirit.*
> *There are different ministries, but the same Lord.*
> *And there are different activities, but the same God*
> *works all of them in each person. A manifestation*
> *of the Spirit is given to each person for the common*
> *good … One and the same Spirit is active in all these,*
> *distributing to each person as he wills. For just as*
> *the body is one and has many parts, and all the parts*
> *of that body, though many, are one body—so also is*
> *Christ. (1 Corinthians 12:4-7, 11-12)*

In his grace (the Greek word for "gift" that Paul uses is literally "grace things"), God has equipped the church to do all kinds of things. But whether we're at the front doing something like preaching or engaged in serving behind the scenes, we need to remember that it is God who enables us to do it and is at work.

"Okay," you might be thinking. "But how do we decide what to do?"

It is important that we work out the kinds of things that God has shaped and equipped us to do. This is a complex process. God doesn't just zap us with particular cookie-cutter abilities—the gifts he gives us come in raw form, needing to be worked at and developed. They also come wrapped up in the strengths and weaknesses of our personalities and character. The New Testament is clear that just because we have the *ability* to do something, it doesn't mean that we have the *right* to do it whenever we want. The fact that Diotrephes (see 3 John 9) liked to "have first place" was enough to persuade John that he shouldn't be leading. This is why God doesn't just leave us to ourselves to work out what we're good at or we'd like to do; this is something that needs to be worked out in conversation with our leaders (or fellow-leaders) in the local church. It's important that we listen to them, as together we work out what we can do and then humbly, confidently get on with it—whether God has equipped us to teach or look after finances or run the sound desk.

But what if we are part of a church where they already have more than enough people to preach or manage the money or look after sound? That's when it becomes obvious that we also need to be people who are ready to do anything. If Christ and his gospel are what matter to us, then no task will be too small or too onerous for us to throw ourselves into if needed. Paul captures this mindset in Colossians 3 like this:

And whatever you do, in word or in deed, do everything in the name of the Lord Jesus, giving thanks to God the Father through him ... Whatever you do, do it from the heart, as something done for the Lord and not for people, knowing that you will receive the reward of an inheritance from the Lord. You serve the Lord Christ.
(v 17, 23-24)

There is no place for being precious in ministry. The church of Jesus Christ is not well served by prima donnas! And yet God has so set things up that he gives the church round pegs to fit into round ministry holes and square pegs to fit into square ministry holes—as together, we work out how best we can serve him at any given moment.

4. BOTH READY TO SHARE OURSELVES AND SELF-FORGETFUL

One of the most basic things about ministry is that it is profoundly personal. It is "people in need of change helping people in need of change".[8] We don't do ministry *to* people or *on* people. Instead, ministry involves speaking the gospel as forgiven sinners to other forgiven sinners as we walk alongside each other. We do ministry as fellow sinful human beings. If we're to do that authentically, then we have to give ourselves to people.

---

8 To borrow from the subtitle of Paul Tripp's great book *Instruments in the Redeemer's Hands: People in Need of Change Helping People in Need of Change* (P&R, 2002).

This is why ministry can never simply be a job. It involves vulnerable self-giving. Paul speaks about the way in which his team operated in Thessalonica like this:

Just as a nursing mother cares for her children, so we cared for you. Because we loved you so much, we were delighted to share with you not only the gospel of God but our lives as well. (1 Thessalonians 2:7b-8, NIV)

Ministry can never be cold or impersonal. It involves sharing our lives. But of course, there is such a thing as oversharing.

It's a matter of delicate judgement how much of our own struggles (and particularly our sin) to share with others, particularly in a public context. Honesty is important, but it is very easy for honesty to spill over into self-indulgence, putting ourselves at the centre of what we say rather than the Lord Jesus. (And sometimes, confessing sin in a Bible-study group or a sermon can be an upsetting distraction to those listening who have been hurt by similar sinful acts in the past.) Likewise, transparency is important, but it is very easy for natural sharing of the rhythms of our life (the antics of our kids, for example, should we have them) to become an unhelpful diversion or even the focus. At the end of the day, while ministry is personal, it isn't actually about us. We are called to self-forgetfulness, not self-promotion or self-preoccupation.

For some of us, our natural tendency will be to veer away from any self-disclosure, which carries the real danger of making us seem slightly cold and inhuman.

That can be for all kinds of reasons, including a lack of self-awareness, unaddressed wounds from our past or a deep-rooted pride. Perhaps we simply desire to make it "all about Jesus"—but we miss the opportunity to show Jesus at work in us.

For others of us, though, we'll have to rein in our tendency to talk too much about either (a) our incredibly vibrant and interesting lives, which can have the effect of making it seem that we are the hero of the story rather than Jesus, or (b) our deep spiritual struggles, which may be genuine but aren't necessarily all that helpful for the people listening, whose lives are quite different to ours. It's a judgement call. We need to remember that ministry is ultimately about *them*, not us, and ensure that we are both ready to give of ourselves and to forget ourselves as we do it.

5. BOTH AWARE OF HUMAN SINFULNESS AND EXPECTANT THAT GOD WILL WORK

If we are to do anything in church, we need to be both deeply realistic and optimistic at the same time. We need to take the depth and extent of everyone's sin (including our own) seriously. But we also need to keep hold of God's spectacular declaration that he is in the business of changing people like us.

Sometimes, we slip into thinking that ministry is all about being nice to people. We talk about the fact that everyone on our team (or in our church) is *lovely* and tell those who help us that they are *so good*. Of course, it's good to want to encourage people and build others up. But that's not the same thing as telling each other that we are nice! The reality is that we aren't all that nice, and neither are they! We are, as we've seen, people who have been forgiven and justified by faith but are also *still sinful* and more than capable of causing all kinds of hurt and mayhem. Remember that when James writes these words in his letter, he's talking about us:

What is the source of wars and fights among you? Don't they come from your passions that wage war within you? You desire and do not have. You murder and covet and cannot obtain. You fight and wage war. You do not have because you do not ask. You ask and don't receive because you ask with wrong motives, so that you may spend it on your pleasures. You adulterous people! (James 4:1-4)

I am still battling with my sinful desires, and so are you, and so is everyone else we'll come across as we seek to serve Jesus. This kind of realism is absolutely vital if we are to do stuff well in church. We won't be caught completely off guard when people let us down. We'll be sad but not shocked when we see others sin. We won't throw in the towel when people cause trouble. We'll also be diligent to have appropriate safeguarding practices in place to protect those who might be most harmed by others' sin. And we'll make sure that nobody, no matter how godly they seem, is above the rules—and that includes ourselves.

But that's not to say that we should be miserable or pessimistic because the Bible also makes clear that our God is in the business of completely transforming people like you and me. A day is coming when we shall see Jesus as he is, so we shall be like him (1 John 3:2). And in the meantime? We can expect the overall trajectory to be up! Nobody is beyond redemption, so we mustn't think or act as if anybody is. No one's sin is too wide or too deep for that person to be beyond God's help—and we may be just the people he uses to give it.

It doesn't matter what we're doing or what kind of gospel service we are involved in; we can expect God to use it to advance his grand purpose to save and change people through his word.

The prophet Isaiah spells out the principle like this:

For just as rain and snow fall from heaven
  and do not return there
  without saturating the earth
and making it germinate and sprout,
  and providing seed to sow
  and food to eat,
so my word that comes from my mouth
  will not return to me empty,
but it will accomplish what I please
  and will prosper in what I send it to do.

(Isaiah 55:10-11)

That means that when we show up on a cold Sunday morning to teach those 7-year-old kids or spend hours vacuuming after youth group or labour through another Bible-study group or endure another music practice, we need to take a firm grip on the fact that as we do the hard yards, God is doing his work, and none of this will be wasted in his economy. That's what both/and ministry is all about.

6. BOTH EXPECTING SUFFERING AND PURSUING JOY

Serving Jesus is often hard but ought never be miserable. We need to remember that.

In some churches, the emphasis is very firmly on the hard bit. We are encouraged to grit our teeth and wait for heaven, putting up with all kinds of deprivation now in the hope that when we get to the new creation, it will all be worth it. In other places, we are urged to live our best life now and given the strong impression that if we trust Jesus, then every bump and wrinkle in our lives will be ironed out, and it will be smiles all the way. And if we're honest, as individuals, we do tend to fall into either the "glass half full" or the "glass half empty" group. But if we are living gospel-shaped lives, then neither relentlessly miserable pessimism nor blithely unrealistic optimism are viable options. Rather, we need to both expect suffering and pursue joy.

One of the striking things about Jesus' interactions with his disciples is the amount of time he spends insisting that life will be hard for them after he's gone. Two blunt examples make the point:

Then they will hand you over to be persecuted, and they will kill you. You will be hated by all nations because of my name. (Matthew 24:9)

I have told you these things so that in me you may have peace. You will have suffering in this world. Be courageous! I have conquered the world. (John 16:33)

And it's not just Jesus. The same note is sounded over and over in the rest of the New Testament (see, for example, 2 Timothy 3:1-5 or 1 Peter 4:12).

Gospel-shaped ministry starts from a place which knows that living for Jesus—and in particular, sharing his message with the world—will inevitably lead to suffering. We need to be prepared for that. But that doesn't mean that ministry should be miserable—far from it—because, in the Bible, acceptance of the inevitability of suffering is bound up with the confident expectation of joy: not just one day in the future when Jesus returns but now in the present as we serve him.

> Consider it a great joy, my brothers and sisters,
> whenever you experience various trials, because
> you know that the testing of your faith produces
> endurance. And let endurance have its full effect, so
> that you may be mature and complete, lacking nothing.
> (James 1:2-4)

In the same way that Jesus himself endured the cross "for the joy that lay before him" (Hebrews 12:2), our lives are to be a delightful and painful blend of suffering and joy. Knowing this will mean that we're unafraid to do hard things. We won't run away from ministry situations that could lead to suffering. But nor will we soldier through them with a masochistic sense of martyrdom. Instead, we'll take the rough and the smooth, looking expectantly to Jesus for the joy that he provides.

All Day, Every Day, for All of Us

There is a sense in which to talk about ministry is really just to talk about what it looks like to live as children of God. As soon as we start to do anything, we need to do it in a both/and way because this is the fabric and the tone of the gospel shaped life. This is the rhythm which shines through in the Gospels, page after page; even when the focus is on what Jesus is doing to rescue us, *the way in which he does it* can't be hidden. So as we serve God, (since Jesus doesn't serve himself) we need to do it like Jesus. This is something that all of us need to take seriously, all of the time. For this is not just about what we do if we are gospel people: this is who we are.

How do I think about ministry?

1 is "I struggle", and 5 is "This comes naturally to me".

I depend on God ////////////////////////////////
5   4   3   2   1

I approach ministry with humility ///////////////
5   4   3   2   1

I focus on using my distinct gifts ///////////////
5   4   3   2   1

I readily share myself /////////////////////////
5   4   3   2   1

I expect people to mess up //////////////////
5   4   3   2   1

I expect suffering to come ////////////////////
5   4   3   2   1

Write down any categories where you have circled 3 or lower:

Can you think of specific reasons why any of these numbers might be low?

\\\\\\\\\\\\\\\\\\\\\\\\\\\ **I work hard to get results**

1   2   3   4   5

\\\\\\\\\\\\\\ **I approach ministry with confidence**

1   2   3   4   5

\\\\\\\\\\ **I'm ready to do anything that's needed**

1   2   3   4   5

\\\\\\\\\\\\\\\\\\\ **I make sure it's not about me**

1   2   3   4   5

\\\\\\\\\\\\\\\\ **I look with hope for God to work**

1   2   3   4   5

\\\\\\\\\\\\\\\\\\\\\\\\ **I pursue joy in the mess**

1   2   3   4   5

Write down any areas that you think you need to address with the gospel:

CHAPTER 5

Both/And Leadership

That's Me in the Spotlight...

For the past twelve and a half years, my day job has been working to equip people for gospel ministry in Queensland, Australia, where I live, and beyond. Over that time, I have steadily grown in the conviction that what God asks of leaders is essentially what he asks of all his people—except that leaders have to do it at the front, in full view of God's people and the watching world. If a member of the church family fails morally or displays deep character flaws, it's not great, but the impact is mainly felt by those directly involved or who are closest to the person. When it comes to leaders, the stakes are higher because the whole church is affected if the leaders are living inauthentically. And nothing damages the church's reputation more than hypocritical leaders. That's why it matters *so much* that leaders lead like Jesus, living a both/and life. And that's why this chapter focuses specifically on leaders and ministry workers.

Whether we're talking about paid ministry (on church staff) or unpaid roles (whether as an elder or in another oversight role or leading a specific ministry in church), being part of the leadership of the church brings a significantly heightened level of responsibility. There is clearly a difference between speaking about Jesus to someone over coffee and preaching to the whole congregation. Similarly, there is a difference between having responsibility for a ministry and simply being part of it. It falls on leaders to set the tone, look out for the whole group (whether other leaders or those being served), and perhaps most of all, to embody the truth which is being proclaimed. That's made clear in a simple statement tucked away at the end of the extravagant sermon that we call the book of Hebrews:

> *Remember your leaders who have spoken God's word to you. As you carefully observe the outcome of their lives, imitate their faith. (Hebrews 13:7)*

The primary role of leaders, like the rest of the body of Christ, is to speak the word of Christ. But for leaders, that is done in a public context and must be lived out in a way which validates the message and gives God's people a visual aid of what faithfulness looks like. As we saw earlier with the apostle Paul (see 1 Corinthians 11:1), leaders are to give us someone to follow by following Jesus themselves.

I'm sure all of us can think of cases where leaders have fallen short of this task. One of the sad things about leadership failures in churches (or parachurch movements) is that the signs that all is not well have almost always been there for a long time but haven't been acted on. In every case that I can think of, it eventually came out that the leader who spectacularly fell into disgrace had not been living a both/and life.

Sometimes leaders stop speaking the gospel to people as everything gradually becomes more and more about them. Sometimes leaders keep speaking the gospel, but they act as if their words (or God's rules) just don't apply to themselves. It's all too easy for leaders to justify their ungodly behaviour to themselves. Or to get completely preoccupied with one facet of ministry (say, adding new families or having a strategy for church planting) so that they neglect others. Believe me, I know: I have battled, and continue to battle, with all of these tensions. In fact, facing up to this challenge takes us to the heart of what it means to be a godly, Christ-like leader. When it comes to leadership, we don't get to choose: *leadership is inherently a both/and thing.*

The Beginning of Both/And Leadership

This is made startlingly clear by the first extended discussion of what we would call leadership in the Bible. In Deuteronomy 17, God anticipates the day when ancient Israel will ask for a king. He says they are allowed to have one on several key conditions:

Appoint a king from your brothers. You are not to set a foreigner over you, or one who is not of your people. However, he must not acquire many horses for himself or send the people back to Egypt to acquire many horses, for the LORD has told you, "You are never to go back that way again." He must not acquire many

*He must not acquire very large amounts of silver and
gold for himself. When he is seated on his royal throne,
he is to write a copy of this instruction for himself on
a scroll in the presence of the Levitical priests. It is to
remain with him, and he is to read from it all the days
of his life, so that he may learn to fear the LORD his
God, to observe all the words of this instruction, and to
do these statutes. Then **his heart will not be exalted
above his countrymen**, he will not turn from this
command to the right or the left, and he and his sons
will continue reigning many years in Israel.*

Notice the conditions that God puts on who can be king
and what they can do. For a start, the king must be an
Israelite—one of God's own people. Second, he must not
"send the people back to Egypt to acquire many horses".
God's people had only relatively recently escaped from
slavery in Egypt—so the king of Israel was not to resort
to using Egyptian military might to strengthen his
kingdom. That would be a sure sign that he was trusting
in horsepower rather than Yahweh. This king (and his
kingdom) was to be different. Third, leadership among
the people of God should be in the hands of someone
whose heart has not gone astray (a single-minded,
wholehearted worshipper of Yahweh) and whose heart
is not exalted (who is humble, expressing that humility
in obedience).

The message of Deuteronomy 17 is that if we start to
get above ourselves, then we are in real trouble. If we
stop listening to those around us, we are in real trouble.

If we start ignoring parts of the truth of the gospel or stop listening to it as it is taught to us by others, we are in real trouble—because, if that's the case, our heart has either gone astray or been exalted. We are no longer leading like the Lord Jesus, who, as we have already seen in Philippians 2, humbled himself to serve, even though he is God and King.

This is what makes godly leadership so daunting and demanding. We don't get to pick and choose between biblical commands and emphases. The rest of this chapter will focus on how gospel-shaped leadership of every kind needs to be a both/and thing.

1. BOTH GODLY AND EFFECTIVE

Instinctively, many of us tend to prioritise *either* personal godliness *or* missional effectiveness. It probably shows in the kind of books we read, the conferences we attend or the preachers we listen to. It's also likely to be reflected in the way we talk about church; are we more interested in measurable outcomes (fruitfulness) or are we more focused on the motivation and integrity of the leaders (faithfulness)? While it's all too easy to default to one or the other, the Bible makes it clear that we need to do or be both.

The exhortation to faithful leadership is found all over the New Testament. Again and again, leaders are called to a life and ministry which is marked by careful, Christ-centred, persistent faithfulness. In 1 Timothy, Paul urges Timothy to "pay close attention to your life and your teaching" and to "persevere in these things" (4:16). What we believe and the way we live matter. This is the foundation of any biblical ministry. We cannot sidestep the need to be godly.

But it is possible—easy, even—to slip into thinking that being godly or faithful is *enough*. Sometimes, we kid ourselves that we don't actually need to think about how we do church or whether our evangelism is effective or whether we are reaching our community or our city or our world. We just focus on being godly and leave the rest to God. But the problem is that while it's clear that we must be godly, it's equally clear that we are also called to bear fruit.

In John 15, Jesus makes this point memorably and forcefully:

> *You did not choose me, but I chose you. I appointed you to go and produce fruit and that your fruit should remain, so that whatever you ask the Father in my name, he will give you. (John 15:16)*

The fruit that Jesus has in mind includes both growth in the number of believers through evangelism and growth in maturity of believers through discipleship. (This is also implied in the Great Commission in Matthew 28:19-20.)

Although God is the ultimate source of growth (1 Corinthians 3:5-6), he also expects us to seek and pray for and work toward that growth. We need to plant and water intelligently, even as we look for God to move. We need to pursue missional effectiveness.

That presents us with another temptation: to become so preoccupied with reaching more people or growing bigger churches that this overtakes the need for godly character on the part of gospel workers. The measurable outcomes (usually the numbers!) trump everything. But the solution isn't to give up on being effective; it's to pursue godly character at the same time.

2. BOTH THEOLOGICALLY DRIVEN AND PRACTICALLY WISE

In a similar vein, leaders at every level of church life need to be both theologically driven and pragmatically astute.

These two things are not at odds. But ensuring that we are both thoroughly biblical in our thinking and effective in our practice is certainly hard work. So often, we pick one, and we end up functionally prioritising sound theology (but giving very little thought to ensuring that church life is functioning well), or we invest our energies in running our ministry brilliantly, without worrying too much about whether or not our programmes and strategies are gospel-shaped.

In the church of the Lord Jesus Christ, leaders must be *theologically driven*. No one is clearer on this than the apostle Paul. In writing to his younger co-worker Titus, he hammers this home. He says that Titus is to be all about one thing—"sound teaching":

> ... *holding to the faithful message as taught, so that he will be able both to encourage with sound teaching and to refute those who contradict it. (Titus 1:9)*

> *But you are to proclaim things consistent with sound teaching. (2:1)*

The word "sound" here means much more than "theologically orthodox" (although it certainly includes that)—it means "healthy" or even "life-giving". The way in which God builds the church is through the Spirit transforming us as a community through the truth of the gospel (see also James 1:18). Theological truth is the fuel which drives the church and the map which guides the church and the musical score which sets the tone of the church. It's not simply that leaders must be well taught but that their theological convictions must mould, shape and motivate their decisions in church. That's what it means to be theologically driven.

But that isn't the end of the story. Leaders must also be *practically wise*.

For some of us, saying that someone is a pragmatist is just about the worst insult we could think of. But dismissing the need to be wise in how we use the energy and resources which God has given us for his glory is just about as foolish as we can get!

Occasionally, I watch a Formula One race. I love the complexities involved in getting an incredibly fast but fragile racing car through 60 or 70 laps of a circuit: the fuel load, the tyres, the set-up of the car, the race strategy (including when to pull into the pits)—they all need to be just right to secure a podium finish. It's neither a matter of "go and drive as fast as you can" nor "take it easy so that you stay safe". Ministry is very similar.

Yes, we must be theologically driven. That will shape our goals and the parameters within which we work. But there are still all kinds of questions we need to grapple with if we are to do what God has asked of us. Yes, it's a both/and thing.

3. BOTH PEOPLE-CENTRED AND ORGANISATIONALLY-MINDED

I know it's almost too obvious to say, but leaders lead *people*. So leaders must prioritise people.

After his resurrection, Jesus tells the apostle Peter three times to feed his sheep (John 21:15-17). Peter then expands on that command in his first letter:

> *I exhort the elders among you as a fellow elder and witness to the sufferings of Christ, as well as one who shares in the glory about to be revealed: Shepherd God's flock among you, not overseeing out of compulsion but willingly, as God would have you; not out of greed for money but eagerly; not lording it over those entrusted to you, but being examples to the flock. And when the chief Shepherd appears, you will receive the unfading crown of glory. (1 Peter 5:1-4)*

To be an elder involves taking responsibility for the people under your care ("overseeing") and doing so "eagerly" and in a Christ-like way. In fact, being a leader in any sphere of church life means, first and foremost, caring about the people. We don't lead churches or organisations—we lead *people*. The apostle Paul (whom no one could accuse of a lack of ambition or strategy) went so far as to compare himself and the other members of his team to a mother feeding a newborn in the way they cared for the Thessalonian believers (1 Thessalonians 2:7).

To lose sight of loving and leading people is to lose the plot as a leader. But it doesn't mean we can just forget about practicalities. Good leaders also need to understand how to make church work. And that means thinking about systems.

When the church burst into life after Jesus' resurrection and the outpouring of the Spirit, it didn't take long before the vibrant community of Acts 2:42-47 ran into some organisational problems. It became very obvious that the apostles were being spread too thinly. A looming "widow war" threatened to bring the progress of the gospel grinding to a halt (Acts 6:1-7). As the church grew, if the apostles were going to keep teaching and leading people, they needed the help of others to take the pressure off themselves. They needed to organise things and put some systems in place.

The church can't afford to have leaders who don't love people, but it's not much better to have leaders who love people but either burn themselves out or are completely ineffective because they can't organise their way out of a paper bag! You probably lean towards one or other of these poles: do you prefer looking at spreadsheets or reading the Bible with someone over coffee? But we really don't get to pick and choose.

4. BOTH LEADERS AND SERVANTS

Leaders *lead*. Whatever shape this takes (and we'll have more to say on this in the next chapter), it means that leaders need to get out in front, show people the way to go and do everything in their power to encourage and persuade people to come with them because this is the best way to go.

You can see this clearly at the end of Hebrews 13:

Obey your leaders and submit to them, since they keep watch over your souls as those who will give an

> *account, so that they can do this with joy and not with grief, for that would be unprofitable for you.*
>
> *(Hebrews 13:17)*

The writer assumes that leaders are taking initiative and taking the lead—because only when they have done this can the rest of us "obey" and "submit" to their God-given authority. This authority is to be understood as part of a deep and expansive care for people, as leaders "keep watch over" the people's souls. A leader's decisions seek the good of the community and the glory of God. But they do need to take those decisions!

For some of us, there are circumstances in which we are too tentative and passive, and our great need is to step up and take some initiative. We find ourselves putting off decisions or talking to a long procession of people before we're willing to make the simplest call. Or we're only ever in reactive mode and never on the front foot with an issue.

Sometimes, we have no problem leading in church but struggle to lead in our own marriage or family. At other times, we may be totally comfortable leading at home but find it much more difficult in the context of our ministry at church. If that's the case, then we need to take this seriously, repent, and turn again to God for the resources he has already given us in the Lord Jesus.

For others, though, the danger is not that we are too tentative but that we get carried away with our own importance. We get a taste for power, and that's really scary.

If we are to lead, we need to make sure that the words of Jesus in Mark 10 are constantly on repeat in our ears:

> *Jesus called them over and said to them, "You know that those who are regarded as rulers of the Gentiles lord it over them, and those in high positions act as tyrants over them. But it is not so among you. On the contrary, whoever wants to become great among you will be your servant, and whoever wants to be first among you will be a slave to all. For even the Son of Man did not come to be served, but to serve, and to give his life as a ransom for many." (Mark 10:42-45)*

The only leaders in the church of the Lord Jesus Christ are servant leaders. To be appointed to leadership in God's church can never mean we leave behind mundane responsibilities to move on to "more important" things. Leadership involves serving the same people in similar ways but *from the front*.

My church, when I was growing up, met in a multipurpose building in the middle of a large housing estate. Every Sunday, after the service, we cleared all the chairs to free up the hall for community activities. For my dad, this was when the character of church members was on display. So when it came to appointing elders, say, there was always a prior question which trumped all others and validated or undermined all other evidence of spiritual maturity: "Does he help with the chairs?" It turned into a bit of a running joke, but there was something profoundly helpful about it, all the same. (And even today, I feel guilty if there are chairs to be cleared and I don't help!)

Of course, putting chairs away isn't a guarantee of servant-heartedness. But thinking that we're too important to do something so menial is a sure-fire sign that our hearts have drifted away from Christ-likeness. Yes, leaders need to be at the front. Yes, leaders should be freed up to perform their role. But Christ-like leadership is servant-hearted. And that needs to be expressed.

Sometimes we don't make it easy for our leaders to keep a firm grasp on this. There may be good practical reasons for giving our leaders special car-parking spaces, spacious offices (with or without oak panelling!), honorific titles and all sorts of perks (like free babysitting or use of holiday homes and so on). But let's remember that the human heart is a very tricky thing (Jeremiah 17:9) and is more than capable of turning well-intentioned kindnesses into fuel for some really unhealthy attitudes.

5. BOTH COURAGEOUS AND SUBMISSIVE
The idea that leaders are responsible for those whom they lead is central to the teaching of the Bible. We've already seen this multiple times. The basic pattern is clear: Jesus is the chief Shepherd/leader, who appoints under-shepherds to share in his work of caring for the sheep (see 1 Peter 5 and also Ezekiel 34,). In most churches, these under-shepherds are those who hold the office of elder or pastor—but even if you're leading in some other capacity, you should be seeking to do so with a similar sense of caring responsibility. And sometimes, that means having tough conversations. To be a leader means having the courage to say lovingly what needs to be said. It means rebuking, correcting and training in righteousness (2 Timothy 3:16).

But that's only half the story. What we sometimes miss is that leaders themselves need to be held accountable.

There are multiple places in the Bible where it is made abundantly clear that leaders need to be team players. It's why Paul tells Titus to appoint "elders" (plural) in every town on Crete (Titus 1:5). Lone Rangers aren't cut out for gospel leadership! They need to listen to, work with and be sensitive to others. And this also means that leaders have to be accountable to one another and the church family for the way in which they lead. Leaders need to be submissive.[9]

James expresses the challenge to leaders with his usual bluntness:

Not many should become teachers, my brothers, because you know that we will receive a stricter judgment. (James 3:1)

Those who teach (and in the New Testament, it seems that all elders have some kind of teaching function and responsibility) carry a heavy responsibility. If they go astray, the church goes astray. One day, those who teach will answer to God himself! And in the meantime? We need to hold each other accountable.

This will work out in very different ways depending on what kind of church we're part of. If you're part of a congregational or independent church, then the leaders are ultimately answerable to the local congregation; if you are part of a Presbyterian or Episcopal denomination,

---

9 I am completely committed to the idea that overall leadership in the church should be "plural"—that the local church should be led by a group of properly qualified local elders. The implications of this will be spelled out in detail in chapter 7.

then your primary accountability will be to a wider group or a bishop. But either way, the following statements are crucial:

- It falls on all of us as church members to ensure that, whatever kind of church or denomination or network we're part of, those in leadership are held accountable.

- If we are leaders, it is our responsibility to willingly submit ourselves to others.

Why does all this matter? Because accountability really matters. Some of us sometimes just want to walk away from confronting hard or difficult things in the church family. We act as if it has nothing to do with us or as if we can do nothing about it. But leaders are entrusted with the care of the flock, and that takes courage. Others of us are quite happy to hold others accountable but don't want anyone to exercise that kind of care for us. The truth is that we all need to be held accountable—and that means accepting and inviting others who ask hard questions, bring a loving rebuke or express gentle concern. Neither neglecting others nor avoiding accountability ourselves can cut it in the kingdom of God.

6. BOTH "ONE OF US" AND "SET APART"

In some ways, it seems to obvious to say it—but leaders must be part of the church. Moses says quite deliberately in Deuteronomy 17 that the king must be part of the brotherhood of Israel (v 15). Congregations should feel that their leaders are "one of us".

Leaders need friends. Real friends. My wife, Fiona, sometimes laughingly reminds me that I have a tendency to count anyone I have ever had two conversations with as my friend whereas she reserves the term for something a little deeper!

The reality is that being in a position of responsibility tends to create relational distance. If you are responsible for holding others accountable, it inevitably changes those relationships. The more prominent the leader and the wider the sphere in which they exercise influence, the easier it is for them to become isolated. The number of people who relate to them normally gets smaller and smaller. That's why leaders need to initiate, maintain and treasure real friendships. In my experience, these friendships come in all kinds of shapes and sizes. *Old friends* are particularly precious—those with whom you have been through all kinds of ups and downs and who have no illusions about you. Then there are *kindred spirits*, who instinctively get how we think and react and who share the same joys—these are a gift from God. *Peers in ministry*, who get the particular pressures that our role brings, are invaluable too. But these friendships have one thing in common—they don't happen by accident, and they take real work to maintain and refresh. But such relationships matter if we are to stay humble and stay on track with the Lord Jesus.

It's natural that we'll grow some of these friendships among the people we serve—our church family is, after all, the focus of much of our time and emotional energy. There is, however, a potential danger: having friends among those we lead opens us up to the temptation of having favourites or being partial. In church life we need to *treat everyone equally*, as James makes clear:

> My brothers and sisters, do not show favouritism as you hold on to the faith in our glorious Lord Jesus Christ. For if someone comes into your meeting wearing a gold ring and dressed in fine clothes, and a poor person dressed in filthy clothes also comes in, if you look with favour on the one wearing the fine clothes and say, "Sit here in a good place," and yet you say to the poor person, "Stand over there," or "Sit here on the floor by my footstool," haven't you made distinctions among yourselves and become judges with evil thoughts? (James 2:1-4)

James' command is addressed to the whole congregation—it is therefore doubly important for leaders to make sure that we don't favour some people over others, no matter how much money they have or how much we enjoy hanging out with them. We are called to love and lead everyone in our care.

Leaders are still human beings and members of the body, but they also have a special role. They are, by definition, set apart to take responsibility, to model godliness and to make decisions on behalf of the church. That means seeing the bigger picture. It means taking everyone into account. It means prioritising the greater good of the group or team as a whole rather than simply considering the preferences of particular friends.

Some of us are quite happy to distance ourselves from people and throw ourselves into the role we've been given. We'll make decisions without worrying too much about whom we might upset. Others of us are much more likely to struggle to do anything which might not go down well with our close friends. Which are you more likely to do? The challenge, of course, is that we don't get to choose. Leaders are both part of the body and set apart to play a special role for the sake of the body.

7. BOTH PATIENT AND URGENT

Finally, leaders need to be both patient and urgent at the same time.

It is no accident that Jesus repeatedly describes the growth of the kingdom in terms of sowing seed and waiting for the harvest (for example, Matthew 13:1-32, 37-43). Waiting for things to grow necessarily requires patience.

All leadership—in fact, all ministry—is aiming at the ultimate transformation of God's people into the likeness of the Lord Jesus, and that means being prepared to do hard yards for the long haul. "Our inner person is being renewed day by day" (2 Corinthians 4:16) as we are gradually transformed by the renewing of our minds (Romans 12:2)—but this really does take time. And because of that, leaders need to be patient:

> And we exhort you, brothers and sisters: warn those who are idle, comfort the discouraged, help the weak, **be patient with everyone**. (1 Thessalonians 5:14)

> Therefore, brothers and sisters, be patient until the Lord's coming. See how the farmer waits for the precious fruit of the earth and is patient with it until it

> *receives the early and the late rains.* **You also must be**
> **patient.** *(James 5:7-8)*

Leaders who are angry and irritable, and who treat broken and flawed people as hindering the advance of their ministry goals, have lost sight of the gospel and the patience with which our Father treats us. Those who are so impatient to see results that it leads to hectoring people do not serve the kingdom well. Leaders need to be patient and allow God to do his work at his pace.

However, that doesn't change the fact that we are called to live as those who know that judgment is coming and that time is short. Jesus himself also uses the metaphor of crop-growing to make the point that now is the time for gospel proclamation:

> *Don't you say, "There are still four more months, and*
> *then comes the harvest"? Listen to what I'm telling*
> *you: Open your eyes and look at the fields, because*
> *they are ready for harvest. The reaper is already*
> *receiving pay and gathering fruit for eternal life, so*
> *that the sower and reaper can rejoice together. For in*
> *this case the saying is true: "One sows and another*
> *reaps." I sent you to reap what you didn't labour for;*
> *others have laboured, and you have benefited from*
> *their labour. (John 4:35-38, also Matthew 9:35-38)*

This note of urgency is picked up by Paul in a slightly unexpected way when he is talking about marriage in 1 Corinthians 7:

> *This is what I mean, brothers and sisters: The time is*
> *limited, so from now on those who have wives should*

*be as though they had none, those who weep as though
they did not weep, those who rejoice as though they did
not rejoice, those who buy as though they didn't own
anything, and those who use the world as though they
did not make full use of it. For this world in its current
form is passing away. (1 Corinthians 7:29-31)*

While we do need to be patient, time is short. We need
to be about the Master's business! We need to get on
with proclaiming the gospel to this generation and
pour ourselves into the life and mission of the church
right now. Gospel-shaped leaders are marked by both
patience and urgency.

God Is the Guarantor

A large part of what makes being a Christ-like leader
so hard is that we tend to lurch between pride and
self-pity. Jesus asks us to spend ourselves for the sake
of others by serving them just as he did. When we
do serve others, however imperfectly, we start to pat
ourselves on the back and fall headlong into pride;
or, if we can't see past the fact that we have served
imperfectly, we start to beat ourselves up, tumbling
rapidly into self-pity!

As leaders, we are engaged in a lifelong battle against
both pride and self-pity. Only by holding on to the
gospel in all its richness can we hope to fight and
keep fighting to the end. It is the gospel itself which
constantly humbles our pride, reminding us that it's not
about us, it's about him: God, and God alone, does the
real work, mercifully equipping flawed people like us
to bring about his good purposes. It is the gospel itself

which lifts us out of our self-pity, reminding us that it's not about us; it's about him: God, and God alone, is the one who enables us to stare our own failures in the face and not crumble, for he is the guarantor of his work, not us. Only God can help us live and lead like Jesus. The great news is that in Jesus, he has already given us everything we need to do this (2 Peter 1:3). And in that, we can take joy.

How do I think about leadership?

1 is "I struggle", and 5 is "This comes naturally to me".

I prioritise godliness ///////////////////////

| 5 | 4 | 3 | 2 | 1 |

I think theologically /////////////////////////////

| 5 | 4 | 3 | 2 | 1 |

I am people-centred ////////////////////////////

| 5 | 4 | 3 | 2 | 1 |

I lead from the front //////////////////////////

| 5 | 4 | 3 | 2 | 1 |

I have the courage to take a stand /////////////

| 5 | 4 | 3 | 2 | 1 |

Others know I am "one of them" ////////////////

| 5 | 4 | 3 | 2 | 1 |

I lead patiently /////////////////////////////////

| 5 | 4 | 3 | 2 | 1 |

\\\\\\\\\\\\\\\\\\\\\\\\\ **I prioritise effectiveness**

1   2   3   4   5

\\\\\\\\\\\\\\\\\\\\\\\\\\\\\\ **I think practically**

1   2   3   4   5

\\\\\\\\\\\\\\\\\\\\\\ **I am organisationally-minded**

1   2   3   4   5

\\\\\\\\\\\\\\\\\\\\\\\\\\\\ **I seek to serve others**

1   2   3   4   5

\\\\\\\\\\\\\\\\\\\\\\\ **I am quick to submit to others**

1   2   3   4   5

\\\\\\\\\\\\\\\\\\\\\\\\\\ **I am "set apart" to lead**

1   2   3   4   5

\\\\\\\\\\\\\\\\\\\\\\\ **I lead with a sense of urgency**

1   2   3   4   5

Write down any categories where you have circled
3 or lower:

Can you think of specific reasons why any of
these numbers might be low?

Write down any areas that you think you need to
address with the gospel:

CHAPTER 6

Both/And Community

Why the Gospel-Shaped Life Is Like Both Cricket and Golf

For me, two of the most relaxing activities on earth are watching cricket and watching golf. I know that you may have other words to describe that prospect, but I think "relaxing" captures it perfectly. In some ways, the two games are very similar; they are both played on grass, take a very long time and involve whacking a ball with a strangely shaped "stick". But in other ways, they are very, very different. Golf is all about an individual whereas cricket is all about the team.

At a golf tournament, over four days, an individual player hits the ball around 260 times (if they are playing really well). There are other people around (like the caddy, who carries the clubs and gives occasional advice, and the backroom team of physios, psychologists, and so on)—but they are really only there to support; no one else on the team hits a shot. It's all about the mental strength, physical condition and skill of the individual.

Cricket could hardly be more different. In the long form of the game (Test cricket, played between nations), all eleven members of the team will play a key part. Over the course of five days, all of them will bat twice. All of them will field, and at any moment, any of them may have a vital role to play. Of course, there are specialist batters and bowlers, but they really do need the rest of the team. When the team wins, rather than one individual receiving the coveted trophy (as in golf), the team celebrates together (in Australia's case, by linking arms and raucously singing the team song in the middle of the pitch!).

Here's my point: living a gospel-shaped life should feel like playing golf and cricket at the same time (so no wonder it often feels so complicated!). If we want to follow Jesus in all the ways outlined in this book, it's about both "me" and "us".

The Challenge of Living a Both/And Life *Together*
With most of the sets of pairs in this book, I'm pretty confident that if we surveyed all the readers of this book, we'd be split down the middle. There would be lots of us, for example, who struggle with overwork and lots who struggle with laziness; lots who struggle with arrogance and lots who are down on ourselves. But when it comes to both taking individual responsibility and being team players, I am confident that the results would be skewed very definitely to one side: towards individualism.

Granted, there may be some reading this who rely too much on other people and who do actually need to take some responsibility for their own obedience and growth. And if that's you, I do gently want to remind you of Galatians 6:5, where Paul reminds us that "each person will have to carry his own load". God brought us to Christ by working in us as individuals, he dwells in us by his Spirit individually, and one day, we will stand before him as individuals.

But I'm pretty confident that the vast majority of us (especially if you're reading this in Europe, North America or Australia) will struggle in the opposite direction; the challenge for us is to embrace the complementary truth that the instant we come to Christ, we become part of his "body"—his family—and *we are in this together*. That's something that we find much harder to take hold of and hold on to.

For several hundred years, most of us in the Western world have imbibed individualism with our mother's milk! That now shows in pretty much every layer and corner of our society—including in the church.[10] That's why in this chapter, we're going to focus on the "us" bit of "both me and us".

Why Accountable Relationships Aren't an Optional Extra (for Any of Us)

From the moment that God speaks to ancient Israel on Mount Sinai, as recorded in the book of Exodus, and calls them his "treasured possession" (Exodus 19:5, NIV), the Bible speaks about the people of God as a community—an entity which is made up

---

10 If you haven't thought much about this, I'd encourage you to read Carl Trueman's book *The Rise and Triumph of the Modern Self* (Crossway, 2020).

of individuals who have responsibility for their own actions but, more than that, who are *accountable* to one another. There is no getting around this. The New Testament gives at least three reasons to think of ourselves as "us":

1. BECAUSE WE'RE A FAMILY

You don't have to look far in the New Testament for evidence of this. The basic form of address in the early church was "brothers" (which, in the 1st century, implied "brothers and sisters"). Then there's the fact that the church is routinely described as God's extended family or household:

> *Therefore, as we have opportunity, let us work for the good of all, especially for those who belong to the household of faith. (Galatians 6:10; see also Ephesians 2:19; 1 Timothy 3:15)*

If we're going to function well as an extended family, we are going to have to love each other. That's hardly a surprise to anyone who has read the New Testament:

> *I give you a new command: Love one another. Just as I have loved you, you are also to love one another. By this everyone will know that you are my disciples, if you love one another. (John 13:34-35)*

Both Jesus and his first followers say this over and over again. (See, for example, John 15:12; Philippians 1:9; 1 Thessalonians 4:9; Hebrews 10:23-25; 1 John 4:7.) The inescapable truth is that we are called and commanded to live in a way which is lovingly enmeshed with other people. Loving people with this kind of family love involves proximity, engagement and accountability.

The trouble is that, for most of us, this feels a bit claustrophobic! Naturally, we like our independence. We want to make our own choices, express our own preferences, and even construct our own reality. We say to others, "You do you!" and expect them to treat us that way too. We carefully create a space for ourselves where other people cannot infringe on what we view as our basic rights or make us feel uncomfortable. The problem with all that is that it is a very long way from how the Bible calls us to relate. We are a family in Christ, who belong to each other and need each other. We are "us"!

2. BECAUSE WE'RE A BODY

In 1 Corinthians 12, Paul takes this a step further when, at some length, he develops the metaphor of the church as a body. This key statement captures his point:

> *For just as the body is one and has many parts, and all the parts of that body, though many, are one body—so also is Christ. For we were all baptised by one Spirit into one body—whether Jews or Greeks, whether slaves or free—and we were all given one Spirit to drink. (v 12-13)*

Through the work of the Spirit, we have all been connected to one another, as integrally as the various parts of the human body. Independence simply isn't an option. Again, we are "us"!

3. BECAUSE WE'RE UNITED TO CHRIST

When we become Christians, we are united to Christ, and through him we are united to everyone else who is "in Christ". This is actually Paul's favourite way of speaking about followers of Jesus, and in part, at least, it's because it captures the fact that it's a "both me and us" thing:

> For through faith you are all sons of God **in Christ Jesus** ... There is no Jew or Greek, slave or free, male and female; since you are **all one in Christ Jesus**.
>
> *(Galatians 3:26, 28)*

This means that living alongside other Christians, belonging to them and being accountable to them isn't an option: it's a given. Of course, we are still personally responsible for our decisions and actions, but we are also permanently, organically bound to each other. We can't pretend we are autonomous beings whose behaviour is just a matter for ourselves.

So How Does This Play Out?

The reason why this is so very important is that we all need two things if we're going to grow in Christ-likeness: we need *encouragement,* and we need *correction*. And where are we to find these two things? Primarily, among our brothers and sisters in our local church.

The normal Greek word for "encouragement" covers everything from an arm around the shoulders to a kick in the pants. It's a full-orbed, all-in, committed kind of thing. The word carries the idea of deep care—of a kind which longs to see the other person flourish and so won't be slow to cheer them on or to call them out when they need it.

The kind of life which we've been talking about through this book is full-on. It's immeasurably rich but also pretty demanding. That's why we need all the help we can get from one another. It's why we need to be sufficiently connected with other people in our church family so that they know us and they care for us enough to get involved in our mess (and vice versa).

This kind of relating is immensely precious, but to be honest, sometimes it can be hard to find in the local church. It's also pretty hard to maintain! So, what if we don't have these kinds of relationships? What are we supposed to do? There is no foolproof method for developing friendships like these, but I'd suggest that we all need to pray that God would give us people to encourage and be encouraged by, to look around church and see the people who need to be encouraged, and then to commit to moving towards whoever God brings across our path.

If we are to be a both/and community, which recognises that we are a collection of individuals who need each other, then that has to be reflected in every part of our church life—including the way in which leaders lead.

The Key Role That Leaders Play

If we are going to be a "both me and us" community, then that has to flow from the top down. It's the job of the leaders to make sure that this kind of loving gospel-shaped encouragement and correction is part of the DNA of the local church.

This starts within the leadership itself. In the Gospels, Jesus selected a group of twelve men to form the nucleus of the new community who would proclaim his death and resurrection. In Titus 1, Paul instructed his assistant to appoint elders (plural) in every town. That's because leaders themselves need accountability, and isolating one person at the top of a "pyramid" is never a smart move. In addition to that, a team of leaders multiplies the number of close connections the leadership is able to have with the rest of the church family and makes it much easier to ensure that everyone is being encouraged and, if necessary, corrected. Shared leadership makes it much easier to be "us". But Paul also makes it clear that the elders need to take personal responsibility for their own godliness. Among other things, each elder that Titus appoints must not be "arrogant, not hot-tempered, not an excessive drinker, not a bully, not greedy for money, but hospitable, loving what is good, sensible, righteous, holy, self-controlled, holding to the faithful message as taught, so that he will be able both to encourage with sound teaching and to refute those who contradict it" (v 7-9).

Full disclosure here: I am a lifelong, convinced Presbyterian. Since the time of the Reformation, we Presbyterians—following the pattern suggested by John Calvin and others—have been all about plurality in leadership. It's in our blood! In Presbyterian churches, the senior minister is only ever "first among equals" as part of a group of elders. Those elders are then accountable to a wider group (called a presbytery), made up of elders from all the other local churches.

These groups are all then accountable to another group (called the General Assembly) drawn from all the churches in the state or country—I told you we take plurality seriously!

The point here isn't that we should all become Presbyterians. This dynamic goes beyond the particular way your church is organised. You can have great structures and no real plurality. You can have lousy structures (or no structures) and take great care to ensure that leaders are held accountable and are always part of a team. What the life of the church looks like in practice can vary immensely. But in every healthy functional local church I know, there is a high level of accountability to the elders and among the elders, and a willingness of the elders to be accountable to others—with a similar culture among any church staff who are not elders.[11] When that dynamic is in place among the leadership, it's a great foundation for a church family which takes both personal responsibility and mutual accountability seriously. The church as a whole will stand a much greater chance of being a "both me and us" thing.

Left to my own devices, I am the kind of leader who wants to charge to the top of the mountain, yelling to those behind, "Who's with me?" In God's kindness (both to me and to others!), I have led alongside those who have gently reminded me that it isn't always obvious to everyone else that (a) taking this mountain is a good idea, (b) charging straight up is the best way to go and

---

11 The question of how paid staff fit into the picture is an interesting one which is beyond the scope of this book. However, I think it's fair to say that a church run by paid staff who are accountable only to themselves is not a biblical model.

(c) we need to take it RIGHT NOW! These fellow elders and co-workers have encouraged me (and sometimes forced me) to listen carefully to others, reason with them and give them time to process. They've taught me to ask for help in planning the route and working out the pace, even when we're all agreed on the objective. I can think of so many times when, if I had got my way, I would have made terrible decisions, but other wiser elders talked some sense into me! They have helped me to prioritise being a both/and leader and, with God's help, to curb my hill-taking instincts (most of the time, at least).

So What Does That Mean for Me... or Us?

As I said earlier, it is possible that some of us need to develop a healthier "independence" by taking ownership of our challenges and problems. And if that's you, I'd encourage you to look to Jesus for the strength and wisdom to start making more of your own decisions. Trust God to guide you as you read his word and listen to your brothers and sisters (and your leaders), and then step out in the right direction. He will help you.

But for most of us, we're wired for independence, and the challenge is to remember that we're part of "us". Living for Jesus isn't a solo sport. We need to move towards our brothers and sisters in church. We need to talk to them about stuff that matters to us. We need to stick around for long enough after church to have meaningful conversations and be willing to be part of smaller gatherings that give us the time and space we need to share ourselves with others for their good and ours.

But that's not all. First, if we're church members, not only has God surrounded us with a loving family of believers, but he has also given us leaders (whether we call them elders or pastors or something else), whose job it is to look out for us, care for us and shelter us from harm. We need to be ready to look to those leaders for care and counsel as we make decisions, and we need to be ready to submit to them when it comes to the life of the church family. Second, as we serve alongside others in the life of the church, we need to remember that we are a family, a body, and brothers and sisters united in Christ—and so we don't get to do things our way all the time! On our own, even the wisest of us don't always know best; we need to learn from each other (even when it's hard!).

And third, if we lead in church—whether as elders and pastors or with oversight for specific ministry areas—we need to remember that even when we are utterly convinced that we are right, we need other people to assess and balance and shape and correct and sift our ideas. We need to remember that we need other people to help us to lead.

Joyful Supervision, Gracious Submission

It's always been hard for stubborn people like us to submit to other people. The record of Israel in their early days as a nation in the wilderness provides strong evidence of that. (If you need persuading, read Numbers 12 – 20!) Moreover, the cultural atmosphere today fosters a kind of fractious, rebellious individualism. Many of us will naturally resist any kind of accountability. We want to forge our own path, make our own decisions and be our own people. But according to the Bible, living a gospel-shaped life means being team players. It means looking out for others and making ourselves accountable to them. It means being "us" as well as "I". It means being willing to be led by others. Remember how the writer to the Hebrews put it:

> *Obey your leaders and submit to them, since they*
> *keep watch over your souls as those who will give an*
> *account, so that they can do this with joy and not with*
> *grief, for that would be unprofitable for you.*
> *(Hebrews 13:17)*

Leaders need help in maintaining this joyful watch as a team together, and followers need grace to submit. We all need each other. That's true on the days when we're delighted we're not alone and on the days when we wish people would just go away. But this is what it means to be part of the church of the Lord Jesus Christ and to live and lead like the Lord Jesus. It's a both/and thing.

How do I think about community?

1 is "Not really", and 5 is "Yes, definitely".

My church family know me and encourage me //////

5   4   3   2   1

My church family know me and correct me ////////

5   4   3   2   1

For members: I'm ready to be led by and submit to my leaders //////////////////////////////////

5   4   3   2   1

For members: I'm ready to serve alongside others and learn from them //////////////////////////////

5   4   3   2   1

For leaders: There are others to whom I'm accountable in a meaningful way /////////////////////////

5   4   3   2   1

For leaders: I work as part of a team and seek input from others //////////////////////////////

5   4   3   2   1

Write down any categories where you have circled 3 or lower:

Can you think of specific reasons why any of these numbers might be low?

Write down any areas that you think you need to address with the gospel:

CHAPTER 7

Why a Both/And Life Is Worth the Effort

Not Complicated, Just Hard

I have an old friend, now gone to be with Jesus, whose regularly repeated mantra about the Christian life was "Don't worry—the first 50 years are the hardest!" And he was right. As we've seen, what God asks of us isn't really all that complicated, but it is demanding. So the big question is "Is it worth all the effort?" Is pursuing a both/and model of ministry worth the work? Is throwing ourselves into living and leading like Jesus worth the pain along the way? My aim with this chapter is to answer that question with a resounding YES!

It's true it would be *much easier* to go for an either/or approach to life, in which we pick the attitudes and behaviours which come naturally to us and award ourselves a free pass on anything which might take too much effort to pull off or keep up. But, as we have seen, that really isn't an option. Ultimately it will neither satisfy us nor honour God. We have been created and rescued, united to Christ by his Spirit and called to be Christ-like—that is, to live a both/and life.

Of course, in one sense, the fact that God tells us to do something should be motivation enough to do it. We shouldn't really need added incentives or require to be persuaded that God's way is best. We really shouldn't—but we do. And God, in his great kindness, piles up multiple reasons for us to embrace his good (if stretching) demands.

There are at least three reasons for us to live this both/and life (beyond the fact that God is God and tells us to): it's the pathway to *authenticity*, to *joy* and to *lifelong growth*.

The Pathway to Authenticity

Most Christians, at some point, do start to wonder if they are the real deal. What God asks of us so far-reaching, so all-encompassing, that when we come up short, we start to ask ourselves, "Am I an imposter?" "Should I really be a leader?" and perhaps "Am I even a Christian at all?"

At one level, the basic way to address that is to preach the gospel to ourselves—that is, to remind ourselves of who we are in Christ: we are those who have been adopted and justified, who are being sanctified and who will be glorified (Romans 8:30). We are saved by grace alone, and nothing can change that. But—and it's a very real and significant "but"—for many of us, there are still those (often deeply buried) nagging doubts. In fact, there's no guarantee that we'll escape this sense of dissonance on this side of the new creation. The question is, how do we deal with those doubts?

This is a real thing for all Christians, but often it can get bigger when we step up to serve more in church. Having a public, up-front role can add to the sense that we are concealing the cracks in our own character. And that's the kind of thing that can keep us awake at night. More than that, in the long term, this can lead to all kinds of pretence, deceit and manipulation.

But there is a better way. It's to live the kind of life we've been describing. The best way to make sure you don't feel like an imposter is to live a both/and life.

Living an Examined Life

Jesus gives us plenty of reasons to take seriously actually living the both/and life. His repeated critique of the Pharisees is essentially that they aren't living that kind of life:

> But woe to you Pharisees! You give a tenth of mint, rue, and every kind of herb, and you bypass justice and love for God. **These things you should have done without neglecting the others.** (Luke 11:42)

The Pharisees weren't the real deal. We see this in Jesus' teaching in the Sermon on the Mount too. Here, surprisingly, the message isn't *You are being far too scrupulous—you don't need to do all that stuff*. Instead, it's that the Pharisees aren't even close to being righteous enough!

In Matthew 5 – 7 Jesus spells out what the real deal looks like, and in doing so he gives us the kind of practical help we need in the pursuit of authenticity. It boils down to three steps.

STEP 1: AIM HIGH

I'm not sure there are many more important passages in the New Testament than this:

> *Don't think that I came to abolish the Law or the Prophets. I did not come to abolish but to fulfil. For truly I tell you, until heaven and earth pass away, not the smallest letter or one stroke of a letter will pass away from the law until all things are accomplished. Therefore, whoever breaks one of the least of these commands and teaches others to do the same will be called least in the kingdom of heaven. But whoever does and teaches these commands will be called great in the kingdom of heaven. For I tell you, unless your righteousness surpasses that of the scribes and Pharisees, you will never get into the kingdom of heaven. (Matthew 5:17-20)*

Jesus says that he has come to make it possible for us to live the fullest version of the life sketched out in the Torah and the Prophets. The life that Jesus has come to offer us is not *less* but *more*. Lots of things change with Jesus' coming, but it isn't that what God asks of us is scaled down; it's ramped up! So, for instance, a dietary system which pointed to the need to be holy is superseded by a lifestyle of holiness; one day a week of Sabbath is overtaken by a life which is all worship, and so on. Jesus' words do not water down the life which God offers us— and in verse 20, he means what he says: "Unless your righteousness surpasses that of the scribes and Pharisees, you will never get into the kingdom of heaven". Jesus says that because he has come, our righteousness can far outstrip the small-minded, box-ticking, rule-keeping pseudo-righteousness of the scribes and the Pharisees— we can choose the expansive, satisfying, God-honouring life that he makes possible.

Which does raise a very obvious question: right now, is our view of what it means to be a follower of Jesus full enough, rich enough, extravagant enough, satisfying enough? Are our expectations high enough? They need to be! Because Jesus makes it possible to choose the beautiful, blessed life—which brings deep joy even in the midst of suffering and rejection—when we are his.

Six times in the section which follows (5:21-48), Jesus says, "You have heard that it was said ... but I tell you..." In every case, Jesus takes what appears to be the scribes and Pharisees' narrow and specific application of the Torah and blows it wide open.

When it came to observing their slimmed-down, concentrated version of the law, the scribes and Pharisees had definitely reached Olympic standard. Tithing herbs? They were all over it. Specifying who was a neighbour and who wasn't? They had a system for that. Doing what you wanted while avoiding *actually* breaking your word? They were experts. They had reduced living for God to manageable standards. But when it came to the big stuff... they hadn't even begun to taste the good life that Jesus came to bring. In their attitude to others (5:21-26), sex and marriage (5:27-32), truth-telling (5:33-37) and their enemies (5:38-45), they had missed the point. Being "children of our Father in heaven" means living in a way which is richer, and more demanding and more extravagantly kind than anything we might have anticipated.

These characteristics are, after all, who God is: "Be perfect, therefore, as your heavenly Father is perfect" (5:48). We can't settle for any less than a life which is marked by the same love and mercy and integrity and beauty of the life of God himself.

STEP 2: FACE THE GAP (AND REPENT)

All that leaves us with a problem: the same problem we've been coming up against through this whole book. There's a gap between what God calls us to and the actual shape of our lives. The great news is that even as Jesus calls us to aim really high (to be like God), he also assures us of an uninterruptible flow of forgiveness and help. But to receive that help, we need to accept that we need it.

That's what Jesus is getting at in these beautiful words from later in Matthew:

> Come to me, all of you who are weary and burdened, and I will give you rest. Take my yoke upon you and learn from me, because I am lowly and humble in heart, and you will find rest for your souls. For my yoke is easy and my burden is light.
>
> (Matthew 11:28-30)

His half-brother James puts it a bit more robustly:

> Draw near to God, and he will draw near to you. Cleanse your hands, sinners, and purify your hearts,

you double-minded. Be miserable and mourn and weep.
Let your laughter be turned to mourning and your joy
to gloom. Humble yourselves before the Lord, and he
will exalt you. (James 4:8-10)

Both Jesus and James are basically saying the same thing: being real means facing where we mess up (whether through simple weakness or sinful choices), owning how we have dishonoured God and hurt others, and humbling ourselves before the Lord so that he might lift us up.

Repentance is a key part of the both/and life. There is nothing new about this insight. For example, the very first of Martin Luther's 95 Theses, nailed to the door of Wittenberg church in 1517 on the eve of the Reformation, said, "When our Lord and Master Jesus Christ said, 'Repent' (Matthew 4:17), he willed the entire life of believers to be one of repentance".

More than 100 years later, the authors of the Westminster Confession of Faith fleshed out what repentance actually looks like in practice. "Repentance unto life" is when (emphasis added)…

… a sinner, out of the sight and sense not only
of the danger, but also of the filthiness and
odiousness of his sins, as contrary to the holy
nature, and righteous law of God; and upon the
apprehension of his mercy in Christ to such as are
penitent, **so grieves for, and hates his sins, as**
to turn from them all unto God, purposing and
endeavouring to walk with him in all the ways of
his commandments.

*Although repentance be not to be rested in, as any
satisfaction for sin, or any cause of the pardon thereof,
which is the act of God's free grace in Christ; yet it is
of such necessity to all sinners, that none may expect
pardon without it ...*

*Men ought not to content themselves with a general
repentance, but it is every man's duty to endeavour to
repent of his particular sins, particularly. (15.2, 3, 5)*

You can see in this searching summary the importance
both of aiming high and facing the gap between the
way we have been living and the life God calls us to. But
perhaps the key phrase in this sweeping definition is
tucked away right in the middle: we are to "turn from"
all our sins "unto God". Which brings us to the third
step in living authentically.

STEP 3: TAKE HOLD OF THE GOSPEL AGAIN

The great danger of emphasising aiming high, self-
examination and repentance only is that our life
becomes depressing and miserable, leading us either
into a heavy intensity or a judgmental smugness. But
repentance is never an end in itself. Repentance is
turning back to God and the gospel.

The kind of repentance traced out above leads to
a renewed sense of forgiveness and security, a fresh
awareness of the all-sufficient grace which God has
already shown us in Christ, and a restored intimate
relationship with the God who has drawn us into union
with his Son by faith. Repentance is an energising,
encouraging, enriching thing. And it is in taking hold

of the gospel again in repentance and faith that we find and display the kind of authenticity which we have been talking about.

The sad reality is that if there is no desire in us to be godly (to aim high) and no willingness to face the gap between what Jesus asks of us and the actual shape of our lives, and above all no repentance and faith, then our lives will never display the kind of authenticity to which God calls us. But it does not have to be like this! God, in his grace, has given us all the resources we need to live with and for him.

Our God calls us to follow Jesus' example in the strength which he alone provides. Of course, we will be reminded constantly that only Jesus can pull off a both/and life, and yet he invites us to follow falteringly, stumblingly in his steps. Our lives will never be perfect, but they will reflect enough of our Saviour's that people will see that we really are the real deal.

If you give yourself to a pattern of aiming high, repenting earnestly, and taking hold of the gospel, then, come Sunday—whether you're standing at the front of church or slipping into the back row—you'll be able to belt out the songs with a clear conscience, knowing that you are not a fake. When you lie awake at night, it won't be because you think you're about to be found out—instead, you'll be able to rest in the fact that you are forgiven and accepted by God. And the marvellous thing is that as we pursue this tough road to authenticity, we also discover that it is the pathway to joy.

The Pathway to Joy

The simple but compelling truth is that living a both/
and life leads to our joy. But don't take that from me.
Take it from Jesus himself:

> *¹ I am the true vine, and my Father is the gardener.*
> *² Every branch in me that does not produce fruit he*
> *removes, and he prunes every branch that produces*
> *fruit so that it will produce more fruit ... ⁸ My Father is*
> *glorified by this: that you produce much fruit and prove*
> *to be my disciples. ⁹ As the Father has loved me, I have*
> *also loved you. Remain in my love. ¹⁰ If you keep my*
> *commands you will remain in my love, just as I have*
> *kept my Father's commands and remain in his love.*
> *¹¹ I have told you these things so **that my joy may be in***
> ***you and your joy may be complete**.*
>
> *(John 15:1-2, 8-11)*

Jesus calls us both to produce fruit (v 2 and 8) and to
remain in his love (v 9) by keeping his commands (v 10).
But it's the result of this that is important to notice here;
Jesus calls us to remain in his love and to produce fruit
so that we might know his joy. The kind of wholehearted,
gospel-shaped both/and life we have been talking about
is the key to joy. God has so set things up that what he
calls us to is good, beautiful and attractive—not least
because it a life *which is filled with joy*.

As before, we can find confirmation of this in the
Sermon on the Mount—this time in the so-called
Beatitudes in Matthew 5:1-12. As Jesus goes up a
mountain and gets ready to map out the shape of the
beautiful life, he's acting like a new Moses, whom God

used to do a similar thing on Mount Sinai in the Old Testament. Jesus opens with the words "Blessed are..."

For the disciples, who had been weaned on the Old Testament, hearing Jesus say the word "blessed" on a hill would inevitably have reminded them of a very different place about 70 km (43 miles) away. Mount Ebal and Mount Gerizim, the twin peaks above Shechem—well-known landmarks on the way from Galilee to Jerusalem—had a special place in Israel's history. When Israel had first entered the land 1,300 years or so earlier, Moses had called them "Blessing" and "Curse" mountains (see Deuteronomy 27 – 28; Joshua 8:30-35). Those hills reminded God's people that they had a choice to make—a choice between blessing and curse. The story of the Old Testament is that they repeatedly chose curse.

Which is where Jesus comes in. He has come to hold out the glorious reality of living the blessed life with him.

When Jesus describes this blessed life in Matthew 5, he draws on the Old Testament at every point: "Blessed are the poor in spirit, for the kingdom of heaven is theirs" (v 3) picks up Isaiah 61—those who have admitted that they need God are on the right track and will share in this kingdom life. Now that Christ has come and the kingdom has broken in, "Blessed are those who mourn, for they will be comforted" (Matthew 5:4), again just as Isaiah 61 promises. "Blessed are the humble, for they will inherit the earth" (Matthew 5:5), picking up on Psalm 37, is a glorious reminder that with King Jesus in charge, the rules have changed for ever—rather than power and wealth being won by the strong, the riches of God's creation will flow to those who are humble and gentle, submitting to God in meekness. As in Psalm 42, it will be those who seek God, hungering and thirsting for his righteousness (Matthew 5:6), who will find satisfaction. The promise of Psalm 18 is fulfilled in Matthew 5:7, as Jesus proclaims, "Blessed are the merciful, for they will be shown mercy". As in Psalm 24, it is the "pure in heart"—those whose focus is set squarely on serving God and him alone—who will enjoy life in relationship with him. And as in Psalm 34 (see v 14, 17) and Isaiah 52 (see v 7), those who pursue God's peace in human relationships are a delight to him.

The picture painted in the Beatitudes isn't a theoretical possibility which remains beyond our reach. This is what Jesus holds out to everyone who believes in him. It is a *rich, counter-cultural, gentle and satisfied life*— everything that God promised in the Old Testament and more. And above all, notice that this beautiful life is marked by joy, even in suffering. At the end of the list of blessings, Jesus says this:

> *Blessed are those who are persecuted because of righteousness, for the kingdom of heaven is theirs. You are blessed when they insult you and persecute you and falsely say every kind of evil against you because of me. **Be glad and rejoice, because your reward is great in heaven. For that is how they persecuted the prophets who were before you.** (Matthew 5:10-12)*

This blessed both/and life will lead to persecution, but it is also the pathway to joy: joy which flows from the reality of knowing that we have lived with and for Jesus and that we have his approval.

The Pathway to Lifelong Growth

I hit an unwelcome landmark recently—for the first time in my life, I was asked to speak on longevity in ministry. When I first saw the invitation, I did a double take. "That's the kind topic that you ask old guys to speak on," I thought to myself... and then it struck me: *I am one of the old guys!* (Thanks to my friend Costa for that unwelcome realisation!)

But it did get me thinking. What has helped me to keep going for the past 30 years of ministry, without losing interest or the enthusiasm for it? Of course, all kinds of things and people have fed into that. But one of the key things has been the challenge of pursuing a both/and life.

This is exactly the point James makes when he insists that we need to be both hearers of the word and doers, and to stick at it:

But be doers of the word and not hearers only, deceiving yourselves. Because if anyone is a hearer of the word and not a doer, he is like someone looking at his own face in a mirror. For he looks at himself, goes away, and immediately forgets what kind of person he was. But the one who looks intently into the perfect law of freedom and perseveres in it, and is not a forgetful hearer but a doer who works—this person will be blessed in what he does. (James 1:22-25)

Being a both/and person takes perseverance. In God's kindness, this is the way he has provided for us to make sure that we don't stagnate or slip into thinking that we have made it. The great goal of our lives is to keep growing and to keep going to the end, continuing to live a godly, consistent both/and life, continuing to grow in Christ-likeness as we live in repentance and faith. This goal doesn't get old. There are always new ways in which to grow.

From time to time, most of us worry about blowing up or burning out or falling away. But the great news is that if we genuinely keep pursuing both/and Christianity, in community, in the strength which God so gladly supplies, *we won't*. We'll make it to the finish line in one piece.

You can see that in one of the most moving passages of the New Testament. Paul is in jail and is very aware that his time is short. In writing to his protégé Timothy, he lays out the kind of ministry he's sought to have and wants Timothy to emulate. It's very definitely not an either/or approach but a picture of zealous commitment to the very end:

> *For I am already being poured out as a drink offering, and the time for my departure is close. I have fought the good fight, I have finished the race, I have kept the faith. There is reserved for me the crown of righteousness, which the Lord, the righteous Judge, will give me on that day, and **not only to me, but to all those who have loved his appearing**.*
> *(2 Timothy 4:6-8)*

This promise is for all of us. Living a both/and life—a life of sacrifice and struggle and joy and perseverance—is the way to make it across the line and receive *together* the prize of the "crown of righteousness" from our God and Father. Isn't that a great incentive and motivation to keep going?

More Than Worth It

In Matthew 25:14-30, Jesus tells the story of three men who are entrusted with their master's money. Two are grateful and show that gratitude by putting the money to work and earning a return. The other just buries the money in the ground. It is those who are both grateful and proactive who receive the commendation of the master. Wouldn't it be foolish of us not to do the same?

Living and leading like Jesus by pursuing a both/and ministry is the most satisfying and joy-filled way to live. It is also the healthiest and most sustainable way to live. And all that is capped by the prospect of hearing the words of Jesus, as he says to us, "Well done, good and faithful servant! ... Share your master's joy." That's what we're aiming for: enjoying God himself for ever.

In a sermon from 1733 entitled "The Christian Pilgrim", the pastor Jonathan Edwards said this:

> *God is the highest good of the reasonable creature, and the enjoyment of him is the only happiness with which our souls can be satisfied. To go to heaven fully to enjoy God, is infinitely better than the most pleasant accommodations here. Fathers and mothers, husbands, wives, children, or the company of earthly friends, are but shadows. But the enjoyment of God is the substance. These are but scattered beams, but God is the sun. These are but streams, but God is the fountain. These are but drops, but God is the ocean. Therefore it becomes us to spend this life only as a*

journey towards heaven, as it becomes us to make the seeking of our highest end and proper good, the whole work of our lives, to which we should subordinate all other concerns of life. Why should we labour for, or set our hearts on anything else, but that which is our proper end, and true happiness?

Why indeed?